From Socrates to STEAM

Student Agency Fuels Potential

Connie Brown, M. Ed.

Gifted
UNLIMITED

From Socrates to STEAM

Edited by: Lindsey Reinert, Ed.D.
Interior design: The Printed Page
Cover design: Kelly Crimi

Published by
Gifted Unlimited, LLC
12340 U.S. Highway 42, No. 453
Goshen, KY 40025-0966
www.giftedunlimitedllc.com

ISBN: 978-1-953360-12-0

Table of Contents

Acknowledgements

I want to publicly thank so many people for helping make this book a reality. First, sincere and limitless appreciation to my husband David, who is my rock, my cheerleader, my illustrator, and my soulmate.

I would also like to extend my gratitude to my amazing (and gifted) children, Allie and Andi, who have taught me so much and so graciously shared their Mom with so many other kids throughout their lives.

To my beautiful granddaughter, Hope, whose entrance to the world inspired me to finally finish a book.

To Gail for being such a great friend and sounding board.

To the literally hundreds of extraordinary educators and students I have encountered over the years: I am so privileged to have worked with so many fabulous individuals in my lifetime and I'm grateful to be part of your stories, as well as to have you as part of mine.

To Kera Walter, DO; Asher Shafton, MD; and Jason Shofnos, MD who collaborated to save my life mid-way through the publishing process—thanks for helping me to be here.

To Joi Lin for the introduction to Molly A. Isaacs-McLeod, and to Molly, for believing in me and sticking with me throughout this very long process—and for publishing my work!

Finally, to Marla Caviness-French, Lauren Stewart, and Jessica Howard, for reading endless pages of discards and supporting me with suggestions and artwork and sanity and laughter. I am forever indebted.

My purpose

About 10 years ago, I read Daniel Pink's book *Drive*. In it, he discusses the secret behind motivation—which he asserts is basically determining the type of person you want to be, the type of contribution you want to make, and then setting to work to make those things true. He suggests constructing a personal "sentence" that defines your end-goal (Pink, 2009). Because I was teaching in a gifted center at the time, the sentence I crafted was this:

"She used her gifts to help others find theirs."

Though I didn't write such a sentence back in 1985 when I first determined to become an educator, looking back I can safely say that the ultimate vision of my work over the past 30+ years has been to support students to thrive in a global society of curious individuals who pursue continuous improvement for themselves, earth's inhabitants, and its resources. And I recognize that this work must start at the grass roots—in individual classrooms in neighborhood schools—where teachers must recognize and inspire students to treasure learning and creativity.

My personal background is that I am one in a family of six children who spent the early years of my life in a then-small suburb east of Denver, Colorado. As a large family with a modest income, we always had enough, but we rarely had plenty. I mention this only because this back story has a significant impact on my life as a teacher. At the age of fourteen, my parents had built some decent equity in the little home they had struggled to buy so many years earlier. When they sold it, we moved to a different neighborhood—a more affluent zip code—and I got an introduction to a different level of middle class in America. In my first neighborhood, I was afforded a fair bit of attention in terms of academics. As a student who was academically advanced in reading, I was always provided with higher reading material (most often reading alone or with one or two other students in the hall), and when I got to middle school, I was assigned the coveted "library assistant" period on my class schedule. But beyond that, my education from kindergarten through middle school didn't offer much in the way of new textbooks or consumable materials for students to work with or even particularly challenging course components.

What I didn't know then was that the schools in my childhood neighborhood just weren't able to offer as much as those in the higher-rent articulation areas or wealthier school districts. Beyond that, there was a certain amount of disdain for school and college and "suits," as my blue-collar neighbors often referred to educated people. While my parents wanted me to go to college, only one of my other 5 siblings had attended college, and I would be the first to graduate with a post-secondary degree. Most of the kids I grew up with did not attend college, and many didn't even graduate from high school. But of the students I graduated from high school with—those in my new neighborhood—almost all (88%) went on to college. Furthermore, the school curriculum there was designed specifically to increase SAT and ACT test scores as well as groom student resumes to catch the attention of college recruiters; something I was very aware did not happen with the kids in my old neighborhood, even though just as many of them were equally bright and creative.

When I began teaching, I had that personal history close to my heart—I wanted to teach all students, yes, but I particularly wanted to offer support to young people who had exceptional aptitude for learning, creatively solving problems, or artistic expression—especially in communities where those students may not be readily identified.

I learned over the first several years in the classroom—from an Arizona border town to a southern California suburb to a return to Colorado, that even beyond the discrepancies in wealth in different communities, many students with an unusually creative mind were not typically recognized for their gifts. Furthermore, I was increasingly made aware that most students felt as though they had very little power in determining their own destiny. Those who were born into wealth felt that they must follow a strict set of directions to maintain that wealth, and those who were not born into wealth felt that there was nothing they could do to change their station in society.

What I observed over nearly 35 years as an educator is, as testing and curricula became more rigid, a sense of disempowerment became even more pervasive. And, from my personal experience, this was remarkably acute in our students who demonstrate the traits of giftedness. Of course, I wanted to teach my students to be excellent readers and writers and researchers, but, more importantly, my desire as a teacher was to support such students with tools and beliefs so that they could have agency over their lives—both presently and in the future.

Even all those years before I knew it, my goal was to "use my gifts to help others find theirs."

After 20 years teaching theatre, communications, and English in both middle school and high school, I took on the role of middle school English/ language arts teacher in a Center for Gifted and Talented students—an application-only, option school-within-a-school. Ten years later, I accepted a position as a resource teacher for gifted and talented in a large suburb just outside of Denver, Colorado. As I began to work beyond my own classroom and with other teachers, my focus began to evolve. My role has shifted from guiding students to instead helping *teachers* find and develop strategies to empower gifted and talented students and engage them in their learning, curiosity, and potential. What I have discovered is that many (if not most) secondary classroom teachers have very little background or understanding about the characteristics or challenges of gifted learners, and even less resources to support such students.

Before I give an overview of my purpose, I am compelled to tell you what this book is NOT.

This is not my dissertation. In some cases, it is even a poor excuse for a research paper. Throughout the book, I will mention/cite the experts that I have learned from, and you will find a very rich list of references at the end of the text. I encourage you to access those resources if you would like to know more about a particular individual or topic. I did not become the teacher that I am in a vacuum—I have read the books and they have influenced me greatly. In fairness, I may or may not have interpreted each of them exactly as their authors would have liked. But they are the ideas that have flavored my career—which was a respectable and gratifying one. This is the book that I wish I had come across as a new teacher or as an introduction to gifted learners.

With that in mind, the purpose of this book has many facets:

One purpose is to introduce educators to a brief history of great teachers and their various philosophies and practices—from Socrates to present day. Certainly, this will not be an exhaustive list, but it will focus on numerous educators who emphasize the importance of putting a student (rather than teachers, administrators, parents, businesses, or even curriculum) at the center of education programs.

Another purpose of this text is to provide intelligent, efficient tools for teachers to plan for and support student agency in their classrooms. Teachers' days are filled with so much more work than most people realize (even more than many teachers themselves realize). Asking them to incorporate strategies to allow for student choice and agency *feels* overwhelming at best and is unattainable at worst. By employing the tools provided in this text, teachers will be able to utilize and/or implement a pedagogy that may be new or unfamiliar to them. Furthermore, having a conversation about student agency (while sometimes challenging) is far easier than incorporating it into classroom practice. The tools provided throughout this text are designed to embed student choice and innovation as well as increase student engagement daily as the teachers work toward the theoretical shift to nurturing student agency.

Finally, this book is designed to help educators of all kinds extend the students whom we reach. Students who demonstrate neuro-diverse traits are often overlooked and misunderstood. Educators must learn to recognize and appreciate the exceptional potential of such students. Only then can they help gifted students find their unique beauty and foster rich gifts for themselves and, as a natural result, for others. While some students can attend centers specifically designed for gifted education (like the one I taught in for ten years), most gifted students are in the general population of neighborhood schools. It is valuable for *all* teachers to recognize the traits of their gifted students so they can best support their special and often mis-interpreted needs. While I would encourage the nurturing of agency for all students, it seems to me that it is *imperative* for gifted students, who may be at a higher risk of dropping out, depression, and anxiety (Colangelo, 2002). Therefore, this book is for all teachers (including parents and coaches) who work with gifted students—not just those who are working in specialized "center" or magnet schools. Our gifted children are all around us!

Hopefully, this work will now reach far beyond the borders of my own district and state and help teachers across the globe find manageable methods to identify and meet the needs of their gifted students.

Note:

Throughout this book, you will see sections calling out various kinds of information blocks. They are marked by these icons:

Tip

Takeaway

True Story

Tool

CHAPTER 1

An Introduction to Agency

To begin to explore the idea of agency, think about the last time you enjoyed a video game—or any game for that matter. If you care enough to analyze what you like about the game, you are likely to determine three central qualities that keep you coming back:

1. **Challenge**—Game makers understand that the very best games have discovered a "sweet spot" of challenge—just enough to keep it interesting, but not so much that a player feels constantly defeated. This applies to any games—from gin or Yahtzee© to World of Warcraft©. The probability of rolling a Yahtzee on your turn is just under 4%, or, more specifically about 1 in every 21 turns (Taylor, 2020). But you will undoubtedly experience other successes (and failures) in those turns, which is what keeps it interesting.

2. **Power**—The second thing that keeps us coming back to games is the sense of power we feel when we defeat an opponent or master a strategy. Video games like Mario Kart© and Grand Theft Auto© keep us coming back because we love the sense of winning the race or gunning down opponents. "We" (at least our perception is that we) are stronger, faster, and more masterful than the challenges and characters we are playing against.

3. **Agency**—Perhaps the most important element, more compelling than even intense power, is the sense of agency that some games give us—we can choose our avatar, our vehicle, our weapons, our path (is that a hidden shortcut?) through the maze of a game. Even in vintage board or dice games, Ellen Langer, a researcher from

UCLA, would suggest that it is not the 5% chance of rolling a Yahtzee that keeps us coming back, but rather the fact that *we* are the ones rolling the dice. Though it probably makes no difference in the outcome of the roll, we find satisfaction in the strength with which we roll or the stylistic flip of our wrist as we toss the dice. The idea that we can develop strategy (whether it is effective or not) gives us a sense of influence and gratification. (Sanger)

This is why people out-grow certain games—like tic tac toe or 'hide n seek' in a small yard. They become too predictable for the more complex thinker. They are games of following the rules—comforting in their mundane repetition of a pattern, but not truly engaging or rewarding. On the other hand, there are some games never seem to get old—even very smart adults can play them time and again, over many years in fact, and still find them engaging and enjoyable because they give us a sense of *agency*.

So what is agency, exactly? In an effort to better define it, I poured through texts by gaming experts like Jane McGonigal ((McGonigal, 2011) and Nick Yee (Yee, 2014). Ultimately, I found the best definition of player agency in digital games on a Question-and-Answer forum for Role Playing Games called "StackExchange". (Tim, 2015)

"Tim" answered the question with this:

1. The player has control over his/her avatar's choices in the game

2. Those choices have consequences to the outcome of the game and

3. The player has enough information to anticipate those choices and consequences.

And though I don't know how credible Tim is, his three-point definition seemed to align perfectly with all that I had read.

If we apply this, instead, to education and our students, agency would be this:

1. The student has control over significant choices in his studies

2. Those choices have consequences in the real world and

3. The student has enough information to anticipate and/or explore those choices and consequences.

Many teachers would suggest that they give their students plenty of choices. After all, they give their students assignments; their students have the *choice* to complete the assignment or not; the syllabus is very clear that students who complete the assignments will earn a certain number of points and those who don't complete the assignments will not earn the points. And they are correct; these are choices and consequences we regularly give to students, and they do, to some extent, give and teach students a sense of responsibility and personal power.

But agency extends beyond such simple choices of "do" or "do not".

As I contemplate agency in the classroom, I find myself considering the ideals of Henry David Thoreau in his text "On Civil Disobedience". In this essay, Thoreau purports that individuals must not act as blind pawns for the larger government but should be very conscious of rules and their consequences. He urges that it is everyone's responsibility to consider the morality of laws that are imposed upon them. In fact, he proclaims that, rather than play a part with an unjust or unreasonable rule, citizens should "break the law…to stop the machine." (Thoreau, 2020).

Both Gandhi and Martin Luther King also encouraged this same type of resistance when they called for peaceful protests against unjust laws. In these instances, we would see individuals intentionally break an unfair law in order to be arrested and thereby allow others to see the unsound rule in action.

Though gifted students as young as middle schoolers may not have a strong knowledge of such ideals and actions, I found that many of them had this same raw attitude about schoolwork—that is, breaking the "law' (i.e., the law would be completing and turning in the work dictated by a teacher or a curriculum) for unreasonable or unnecessary—or even un-interesting—assignments, is a form of civil disobedience that is worth the price. In other words, they are willing (consciously or unconsciously) to fail a class or, eventually, drop out of school rather than conform to a system that doesn't have meaning or make sense to them.

Let me clarify—I am not suggesting that these students were influenced by the words of any of those great thinkers. In most cases, they hadn't had much exposure to those historical figures yet. I am just explaining that in my own experience, I watched a fair number of students push against the system of school—if the math was clear in their head, they neglected (or refused) to show the work; if they remembered the dates, they did not make the flash cards; if they knew the vocabulary terms, they would not do the word search.

It would be fair to argue that some of these behaviors are the result of a lack of executive function (many gifted students struggle with time and materials management).

Most of my students benefitted from exposure to organizational and time management strategies, which will be discussed later in this book. For more support with executive function skills, see the work of Richard Guare and Peg Dawson, who have created the book *Smart But Scattered* (Dawson & Guare, 2009).

But I am saying more than that. In my experience, when students didn't do the assigned work, it was because the work was (again, consciously or unconsciously) not a priority to them. They were "choosing" to fail assignments and sometimes a whole class because they could not find a personal connection to what they were learning.

Unfortunately, secondary students can not truly have enough information or life experience to explore the consequences of disengaging from school before they make such a choice. And frankly, suggesting that such consequences are reasonable for young people is irresponsible. Especially if we can entice the students to learn important and necessary skills by simply offering choice in topic, product, process, or assessment as they navigate their education.

This is not intended to disparage teachers—in fact, just the opposite! The strategies suggested in this text are intended to celebrate teachers and offer some simple solutions for providing more agency in the classroom. When we provide student voice and choice to be a central part of their learning, we will engage and empower those who may otherwise feel disenfranchised. It is our job as educators to foster this exploration in our students and this text is intended to help teachers do that.

Before writing this text, I had the opportunity to present some of the ideas in it to several different audiences of educators in my district and my state. Admittedly, it wasn't a huge number of querants—just under 150. Nonetheless, I took advantage of my captive audiences and asked this question:

Thinking back to the most important teacher(s) in your life, which single statement most encapsulates what you appreciate about them?

1. They taught me a lot of facts, ideas, and skills

2. They encouraged me to be creative

3. They helped me excel on tests

4. They were very organized

5. They seemed invested in my success

Before reading their answers, I encourage you to consider your own response. What was it that drew you to your most important mentors? And how has their action or influence impacted your life since knowing them?

From my informal data, the answers came back with about 70% of participants responding, "They seemed invested in my success."

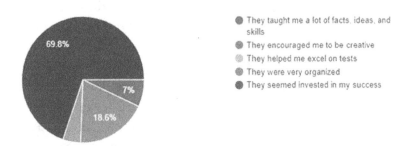

A little less than 20% indicated that they appreciated their teachers for encouraging creativity, about 5% answered each A (they taught me a lot of facts, ideas, and skills) or D (they were very organized), and no one has answered "They helped me excel on tests."

I would say that, when I entered my first classroom in 1987, virtually all my colleagues were interested in teaching students lots of facts, ideas, and skills and most seemed genuinely interested in their students' success—which we measured by whether or not they graduated high school, and if they were caring or happy people.

While I would argue that this is still true today (most of my colleagues seem genuinely interested in their students' success) many teachers tell me that they gauge student success—and their own success as teachers—by the state standardized test scores.

The sheer volume of state testing in our schools implies that student success can be measured by these scores alone. The policies created by that belief has pushed many of our schools to become institutions driven by test results—perhaps with the unintended consequence that our students are learning to look outside of themselves for affirmation. My belief is that they would be better served to learn to know themselves, follow their curiosity, or pursue their passions. Unfortunately, these are attributes that are not easily measured on a test.

There are many roads to success—and while some of those paths may require written or multiple-choice tests, many (if not most) do not; or in any case, the test is not the focal point. In today's educational climate, there are many tools and strategies available to teachers to organize lessons that teach a lot of facts, ideas, and skills.

This book is about going beyond the testing element of teaching and giving the students a voice in the direction of their learning. In my perfect world, education is something that is *driven* by students, not something that *happens* to students. From my perspective, this element of agency is what our gifted students, especially, need in *addition* to the learning of facts, ideas, and skills. When we get to know our students well enough to feel personally invested in their success as a human being, good teachers will unquestionably provide them with the skills and opportunities necessary to reach literacy and employability; great teachers will help them reach their fullest potential.

Teachers are in various stages of understanding this concept of being personally invested in their students' success (and what 'success' means). Before delving further into this text, begin defining for yourself what student success means to you and how invested you are willing to become in helping your students pursue their potential.

Then consider the depth to which student agency can be nurtured in *your* classroom, and why it will matter if agency is nurtured—or, conversely, what is the result to students and communities when agency is neglected.

CHAPTER 2

Understanding the Gifted Student's Unique Need for Agency

What does it mean to be gifted? And why do gifted students need agency more than other students?

The answer to the first question (what does it mean to be gifted?), at least for the purposes of this text, is *maybe we don't exactly know.* But the field is not at all new and there are many working definitions to choose from.

Lewis Terman revised the original Binet Intelligence test in 1916 (now Stanford-Binet) and was long considered a leader in gifted identification (Leslie, 2020). Based on this test, children who have an IQ between 120-140 are rare and identified as having "Very Superior Intelligence". (Terman, 1916)

Others, like Joseph Renzulli, propose that gifted identification must rely on more than one data point and that, rather than a single test, giftedness is demonstrated across multiple facets. Specifically, he introduced his Three Ring Conception of Giftedness (Renzulli, 1984) to support the idea that students are truly gifted when their above level ability, task commitment, and creativity in a certain area intersect. Those areas can be identified by a single test taken over time OR a compilation of tests and performance.

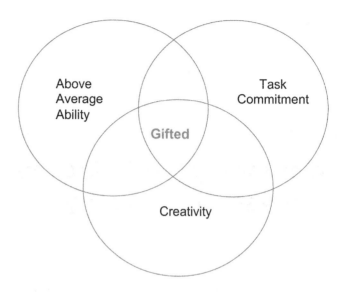

Renzulli Model

For our purposes, I will adhere to the definition provided by the National Association for Gifted Children:

> "Students with gifts and talents perform—or have the capability to perform—at higher levels compared to others of the same age, experience, and environment in one or more domains...many consider children who are in the top 10 percent in relation to a national and/or local norm to be a good guide for identification and services."

Furthermore, the Association specifies: "Students with gifts and talents:

- Come from all racial, ethnic, and cultural populations, as well as all economic strata.
- Require sufficient access to appropriate learning opportunities to realize their potential.
- Can have learning and processing disorders that require specialized intervention and accommodation.
- Need support and guidance to develop socially and emotionally as well as in their areas of talent." (What is Giftedness, 2019)

Though this is a very comprehensive definition, there is no guarantee that all students who are gifted are accurately identified as such. In the United States, and certainly in my home state, gifted criteria are generally based on scholarly achievement (that is, teachers and specialists in schools and districts use a body of evidence including state standardized test scores and norm referenced cognitive batteries to identify a student as gifted and talented). In my experience, while the classroom and resource teachers who are tasked with reviewing this data take great pains to try to separate natural talent (innate potential) from nurtured ability (what a child has learned via private or home-privileged lessons), it is extremely hard to distinguish between those two means of talent; students who are naturally talented but haven't been nurtured in that talent area are sometimes (if not frequently) missed. Beyond that, some students may have difficulty overcoming language barriers while others struggle to overcome a learning disability, which also creates disparities in identification.

What this means for teachers is that unidentified gifted students are probably sitting in your classrooms, and recognized or not, they likely have educational needs that are not currently being met.

To be explicit: Do not be stingy with gifted support.

The students in your classroom who are performing or indicating ability better than 90% of the rest of their classmates should be provided with extensions, in-depth social emotional supports, and other tools typically provided to identified gifted or talented individuals.

That 10% of your students who seem to have a spark or ask more questions or develop unique or unusual ideas should be provided with extensions, in-depth social emotional supports, and other tools typically provided to gifted or talented individuals.

In other words, any student who seems atypical in terms of energy or curiosity or behavior—regardless of either cognitive or achievement scores or even official "GT" Identification—should be provided with extensions, in-depth social emotional supports, and other tools typically provided to gifted or talented individuals. (We will look at many of those supports in chapter 9 and other places throughout this text.)

And we must take it beyond that. When we have a student who is reserved, unengaged, angry, or otherwise finding little success in the classroom with his or her peers, his teachers, or the curriculum, we must investigate further, not only with tests to identify if the student has learning deficits, but also to determine if the student is gifted. Sometimes this can be done with testing, but more often at the secondary level, I have found these students are better identified in action. Rather than simply administering a specialized test for cognitive abilities, lead the student to a project that will grab her attention and catapult her into further learning. From my perspective, especially at the secondary level, it is more important that the student receives the accommodations he needs than that he is identified with the label of gifted and talented (though such identification may help students and their teachers better understand and support their neuronal divergence as they progress through school and life.)

For some students, this may come in the form of working on a school play or with the technology club. Others are harder to crack though and need something that feels less school-like. It may be a video contest (for cash prizes!) or a junior internship at the local credit union. One student finally found and demonstrated his giftedness by pursuing sponsorship for his skateboarding, while another launched a podcast. In all these cases, teachers made a point of not only learning about the interests and aspirations of their students, but they also asked the students for direct input into their course of studies.

When we start with "What would you like to learn, do, or create?" we can lead the student to the most valuable tools to support their success.

Why do gifted students need more agency than others?

The answer to the second question posed in this chapter (why do gifted students need more agency than others?) is also murky. The truth most likely is that gifted students do not necessarily require *more* agency than other students—but in my experience they do seem to *feel the lack* of agency more acutely than others.

Before I understood the value of offering authentic agency to my students, I believed that giving students a few options for an assignment was giving them appropriate choice and if they still didn't do the assignment, I often (unfairly) assumed some pretty negative things about them.

For example, many teachers with whom I work will assign research papers on specific topics or individuals—for example, as a summative assignment for a middle school social studies unit, a teacher may direct students to "Create a presentation explaining three key components of Manifest Destiny and demonstrate how they affected the societal attitudes of 19th Century America." I have found that, although there may be some grumbling about the difficulty of the work, most students will comply with getting this kind of assignment completed. However, sometimes there will be a student who simply refuses to do the assignment—he may be passive aggressive about it, or she may be overtly hostile. Often, I find that the students who respond in this manner find such an assignment to be counter to what they found important about the unit. They are usually unable to articulate this frustration on their own, but when pressed, they say they would rather explain a connection to modern day, or maybe they would prefer to write a song or create a sculpture that embodies the true essence of their learning.

Some teachers I've worked with have just allowed such students to take the failing grade. They may argue that these are simply students who didn't engage in the unit. From my perspective, though, their reluctance to complete a concrete, mandated assignment may instead be a symptom of their gifted minds and overexcitabilities.

According to Dabrowski's Theory of Overexcitabilities students with 'advanced personality development' typically demonstrate the five forms of overexcitability (psychomotor, sensual, intellectual, imaginational, and emotional) as well as a strong autonomous drive to achieve individuality (Lind, 2011).

What that means is that most gifted students will respond exponentially to a stimulus input, and they will also *need* to feel that learning has a purpose for them. They are more likely to learn as they are creating or experiencing a stimulus than they are when simply recording facts or practicing a skill.

Here are some examples of Dabrowski's Overexcitabilities and the challenges they may present: (Lind, 2011)

Psychomotor	When a student is experiencing this type of over-excitability, he may have an excess of energy and must be provided an outlet for this excess. Often, this energy will manifest as nervous tics, nail biting, pacing or dancing, exaggerated gestures, or impulsive behaviors.
Sensory	This may be expressed in the manner in which sensory pleasures or distractions are experienced. For example, vibrant sounds, colors, or textures may be sought for the pleasure they bring, or tags in a piece of clothing, the tightness or looseness of a pair of shoes may be unbearable, or a particular sound, like someone breathing or chewing, may feel intolerable.
Intellectual	This overexcitability is associated with an intensity of thought, curiosity, and inquiry. People who experience this are often more engaged with the pursuit of information than with the expression of it. While some may seek learning, most are just needing to be immersed in the acquisition of information and truth, and academic achievement takes a back seat to this greater endeavor.
Imaginational	This is a free play of creativity, ideation, and invention. For example, when someone with this overexcitability sees a picture of a person hiking on a mountain path, they may fear that the person will fall off the mountain. This can result in frequent daydreaming and/or distractibility.
Emotional	According to Dabrowski, this is the most commonly manifested overexcitability and it can include extreme anxiety related to physical pain or fatigue, concern with death, shyness or self-consciousness, fear, guilt, and depressive or suicidal moods.

Dabrowski additionally suggests that such students also experience an autonomous factor. This factor drives gifted students to not only behave in ways that feel more authentic to their true selves but also directs them to pursue only qualities or desires that align with their innate values (Tillier, 2009).

The implication of the "autonomous drive" is that, due to their over-excitabilities, students may not be willing to engage in the material being presented in class because they are focused on (or even consumed by) a different idea.

If we change our mindset, each of these challenges can be valued as strengths rather than deficits, and the teachers and parents I've worked with who direct their students to explore these manifestations as "superpowers" generally have great success with building healthy people. In any case, for me, beyond any other explanation, these over-excitabilities—these extreme responses to even mild stimulus—can help us make sense of our gifted students' need for voice and choice in their educational pursuit.

Now that we've established a hard-wired need for gifted students to experience a sense of autonomy (and the agency to achieve it), let's return to our definition of student agency:

1. The student has control over significant choices in his/her studies

2. Those choices have consequences in the real world and

3. The student has enough information to anticipate and/or explore those choices and consequences.

So how can we provide significant choices in their study?

In many cases, the secondary level gifted student already knows how to read and possibly is effectively using context clues to determine the meaning of new words.

But even students who don't know how to read well (for example, perhaps they are second language learners, or they have an identified learning disability) may have strong critical thinking skills that take them beyond the prescribed articles and worksheets being fed to 'catch them up.'

Billy Preston's song begins: "I got a song/I ain't got no melody" (Preston & Fisher, 1972). This often feels like the case with gifted students who are on the Autistic spectrum or who otherwise experience over-excitabilities. Sometimes the "song" is in them, but they have no "melody" with which to make it coherent. In other words, they are very intelligent, but they lack the social and communication skills to access or share their unique gifts with others.

Carter (not his real name) was one of those students. He had scored quite high on early cognitive tests, but he seemed to have little interest to do well with most of the work he was given in school. In the year before he started middle school, his mother and his 6th grade teacher reached out to us to let us know he was planning to attend our school. His teacher knew our program and instructors, but his mother had never met us—never sent a child off to middle school before— and she was very nervous. She had good reason for concern. Carter was on the extreme end of the autism spectrum: he was intensely anti-social, and he was known to "wander" in his elementary school—that is, he would sometimes take his own route from a classroom to the library or occasionally not make it to the lunchroom with the other students because something along the way had caught his attention. His mother worried that he would get lost—both literally and figuratively—at our school. In our first meeting with Mom, she showed us Carter's baby picture and wept, "This is who I see when I look at my son—and I'm trusting you to help me take care of him."

Despite the pressure of his idiosyncratic needs, we were excited to have Carter coming to us. He was an interesting case and different from most of the students we had worked with before. Personally, I was just beginning to realize that our work in the Center School was more than providing a rigorous curriculum, and this student would be a test for us. He was a perfect example of an asynchronous learner—he was quick to learn some things, but extremely far behind in others. He could read exceptionally well and talk at length about scientific theories, and he could compute math in his head, but he had yet to write a complete paragraph in any class, much less an essay, and showing his work on simple algebraic problems seemed (to him) like a waste of time. The value of being able to communicate great ideas in any manner besides speaking was lost on him.

Carter taught us much about teaching to the "whole child". For one thing, he needed to move almost constantly. Sitting still made him anxious and unfocused, but if he rocked or stood and paced a little, he could follow a lesson for quite a long while—longer than many of the other students in class. Before Carter, a few of us were willing to let students stand in the back of the room during a lesson, but most of the team believed that students should be seated for the class period—unless the assignment dictated moving. With Carter, we all had to let go of that teacher preference. Furthermore, Carter didn't seem to have a clear idea about boundaries that he couldn't *see*, so we started using painter's tape in our rooms to indicate the areas where he (and eventually others) could move. His elementary teachers had done a great job of teaching about "bubble space" (which indicated an invisible bubble that people need for personal space) so anytime he got too close to another student or their things, we could all use that prompt to politely redirect him. He had a hard time interpreting facial cues, so we began to incorporate silent video clips as mini lessons to help him learn how to "read" emotions. (It turned out that this strategy helped MANY of our students, who later reported that they also didn't know how to read facial cues!) These new instructional goals were so effective for so many of our students that we began incorporating them into our everyday lessons and still use them.

One day, as I was passing the library media center, I came upon Carter and his science teacher in the hall. Carter was wailing, rocking back and forth in a ball on the floor, snot running from his nose and spit from his mouth. His teacher was clearly frazzled. Since I had no students at the time (it was my planning period), I sent the teacher back into the library with her class. At first, I didn't know what to say. The "director" teacher in me wanted to tell Carter to calm down and straighten up, that this wasn't very hard—all he had to do was find the sources online and write them down, for goodness sakes! Sometimes people must do things they don't want to do, right?

But this was clearly VERY hard for Carter. He wasn't just having a temper tantrum because he wasn't getting his way. He was physically uncomfortable, and nearly inconsolable. Maybe I just needed to let him get through this angst?

Due to the volume and spectacle of his outburst, this didn't seem very productive. So, I sat down with Carter, on the floor, in the hallway. We managed to do a "5 Senses" redirect—where the person having a panic attack names five things he can see, four things he can feel, three things he can hear...etc.—and he was able to calm down. I asked him what happened, and he said,

"She wants me (gasp) to make a list of three sources from my research. (Sob) I hate lists!!"

He was starting to calm down, so I said, "Carter, I can see that this upset you very much. I'm sorry you are upset, because it must be awful to feel like you do right now."

He nodded and sucked in some air.

"I understand that you really don't like lists."

He nodded again.

"I hate them," he whispered.

Carter was calm enough to think a little bit by now, so I asked him. "What shape DO you like?"

He hugged his knees and stared at the ground. "Circles. I like circles."

So, I drew a circle on his page and asked if he could write his sources in that instead. Initially, he was worried that he would get in trouble, so I labeled it "Sources" in the middle and told him to remind the science teacher that it was a "Circle Map" —which is a structure we often use in school. This seemed to satisfy him, and he went back to class and found not three but seven sources for his research project!

This is an example of flexibility that helps students like Carter thrive. It takes a minor adjustment on our part, but it makes an enormous difference for them. And I know for certain that his science teacher would have suggested it, but it hadn't occurred to her that he would take her direction (make a list...) so literally. Sometimes, as educators, we have to say from the start, "Make a list—or whatever graphic organizing shape you like—to collect at least 3 sources for your research today."

Another strategy we learned to use with Carter was writing in picture frames. Because he had such rocky skills in writing, we got in the practice of having him compose his work in the form of a google presentation—at first typing one sentence per frame and, gradually, building from there. As a seventh grader, Carter spent a good deal of time inserting images and animations to his 5-15 frame "paragraphs," and there were days when we worried (because his focus wasn't on composition) that we were making a mistake. But by mid-eighth grade, Carter was writing essays with ease, and without the aid of google presentations. His work became fluid and coherent. It was a slow but steady process, and it worked. His writing scores moved from 'unsatisfactory' to 'advanced' from 6th grade through 8th grade.

People ask all the time if the practices I profess—especially around flexibility—don't "coddle" or even "enable" the students. My experience says no. Sometimes as educators, we believe our goal is to make students conform to the rules. We justify this by saying that they will have to do "this" to get into college or they will have to do "that" to hold a job. While this is partly true (jobs generally require us to arrive and leave at certain times as well as perform certain duties while we are there), it is a simplification of the reality. For a student like Carter (and there are many variations of Carter), helping him break down big ideas into simple parts and analyze them and helping him understand the value of effective communication were the critical issues to his success.

For what it is worth, Carter went on to perform very well in high school (where he continued to have supportive teachers) and earned an excellent scholarship to the University of Colorado, where he is currently studying Engineering. His ability to do this wasn't a result of his teachers "changing" him to fit in and follow the rules. He has been able to flourish because we honored who he was and built upon his strengths. To bring this idea full circle (as a nod to Carter, who likes circles so much), we gave him a melody for his song—we've allowed him the skills to share his gifts with the rest of the world.

Perhaps you have a student like Carter, whose ability to see patterns is so innate and strong that she already intuits how a life cycle or an ecosystem works after reading one or two articles or conducting one experiment about it. Maybe he already knows how to multiply and divide large numbers—yet, our curriculum often requires us to drag these students through study units that reverberate these concepts to the point of boredom and drudgery. Where is the significant choice for these students? Must they be forced to read the same text as everyone else in the room (even though they may have read it two years ago?)

What choice is left to them beyond doing what feels like busy work and turning it in if they want the credit? Such a choice doesn't feel consequential to someone who is just going through the routine for the sake of a grade because, frankly, it is not. Even if one makes the argument that the grades will get a student to college, the significance of this point eludes many students—especially before their junior year of high school—and many of our most gifted students have been talked out of a college track completely by then anyway.

So, we must ask ourselves, how can school be meaningful for students who already have a pretty good (or even excellent) grasp of the material that is being presented? And how can we help them move past a tedious syllabus and into a realm of meaningful study and learning and creating?

One great place to start is with George Betts' Autonomous Learner Model and the more recent Resource Book that complements it (Betts, Carey, & Kapushion, 2017). In his model, study is designed to follow a continuous series of orientation to giftedness, individual development, enrichment activities, seminars, and in-depth study. This can align directly to enrichment programs or be integrated into core subject course work.

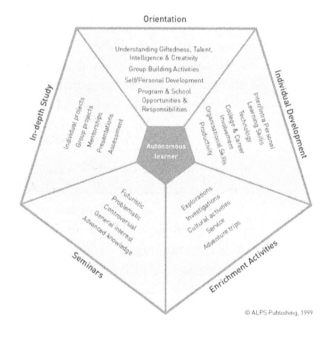

© ALPS Publishing, 1999

The gist of Betts' work is that the students will be more involved in pursuing curiosity and sharing their ideas and creations than if they are simply busy learning a prescribed set of facts, vocabulary, and skills. My own classroom and observing other teachers who use the Autonomous Learner Model as a framework for their classes has shown me that, for gifted students, learning about themselves is engaging and inspires them to bask in the journey of discovery.

There is much work to be done to truly pursue a global pedagogy that nurtures student agency and encourages all students to actualize their potential. There are many people around the globe who are working together to make such a vision come to pass. However, for the purposes of this text, we are focusing individually on teachers (including parents and coaches), schools, and districts—creating a bottom-up process of improving our educational practices. That is not to say that there aren't many, many people and groups who are working from the top down, affecting policy changes, standards, and funding. Those groups are incredibly important and necessary. Their work must happen in tandem with the work of districts, schools, and individual teachers in order to create true and meaningful change in the approach to education.

Gifted students are present in all populations of our society, and they have special needs which must be provided for. Most notably, their natural tendency toward overexcitability can prohibit them from accessing instruction in the same manner as their peers. Students who are experiencing these overexcitabilities may be distracted by physical, sensory, or emotional agitation, or they may be consumed by intellectual or creative thoughts. One way to remedy this is to employ teaching models that nurture autonomy, support them in following their line of thinking, and help them explore self-awareness.

I have been fortunate enough to travel around the state, the country, and even overseas to present and learn about teaching designs that work—especially for gifted learners—but I don't pretend to have all the answers. In fact, I still have a lot of questions, which is what took me on the journey of this work. I wanted to explore how the educators I have studied might have included agency in their pedagogy, as well as discover common threads across time.

I started with Socrates, the father of Western philosophy.

Chapter 3
Agency Isn't New
(Socrates vs Sophists)

To truly grasp the philosophical switch from education as a filling of a bucket to education as a journey of actualization, we need to travel back to around the 5th century BCE, which is the time of Socrates. In other words, student agency isn't a new concept. But rather than considering this discussion a re-packaging of an old idea, we will approach it as an evolutionary process. Hopefully, there will be at least one mutation that makes strategies for supporting agency significantly fresh and relevant to current times.

As we move back in time, imagine the world's oldest moving picture. If you can't imagine it, you can easily find a clip of it on the internet. It's called "Horse in Motion" and it was made in 1882. (Hunt, 2017) Interestingly, it wasn't designed to be a motion picture, per se. Rather,

some people were debating whether all four of a horse's hooves left the ground at one time and wanted to prove the correct answer. So several cameras were set up to film the motion of a horse while in full gait. This short film was the result.

Everything that has happened in the field of motion picture starts there. Think of the questions that may have been explored in the time since: How can we get such a picture using only one camera instead of several? How do we expose only a small piece of film to the light in every second without ruining the other film on the roll? How do we tell a story with the film? How do we make it big enough for lots of people to see at once?

Then, think of how those questions exponentially evolved over time. How can we add sound? Color? Effects? 3D? CGI?

And think of the ethical questions that have come into play in the 140 years since that film was made: Do we use film to capture reality, or create it? What is the balance between truth and story? To what extent may a filmmaker interfere with—or neglect—the outcome of what he is filming?

My point is not to teach the history or ethics of film, though. Rather, this information is presented as an invitation for the reader to consider the barebones simplicity of that first film and then, in the spirit of the Depth and Complexity© framework, consider how things—all things—change over time.

In turn, consider the barebones simplicity of earliest education—which was likely offered from elder to young in a family group many thousands of years before the dawn of historical civilizations. Direct instruction about very specific skills like hunting and preparing food, about creating shelter and keeping it habitable. Even those simple ideas had to improve constantly in order to develop larger and more sustainable societies, like Ancient Greece, that could produce a new thinker, like Socrates.

When I consider the teachings of Socrates, I like to think of him in images much like that horse in motion—he is grainy, in black and white. I realize that many people today may imagine Socrates by his inclusion in the movie *Bill and Ted's Excellent Adventure*, where he was depicted as standing among "many steps and columns," sagely explaining that our lives were like sands in the hourglass. However, I still imagine him as a granular moving-picture profile, and I would maintain that the character we know as Socrates best demonstrated his wisdom by proclaiming that he "knew nothing."

Before Socrates, the other "teachers" we know of were the Sophists. Sophists were supposedly "experts" in a particular field (or a particular set of fields). More often, though, they were simply very good speakers who came to Athens to be hired on as private tutors for wealthy families. Though they called themselves 'wise' they were more often just good at rhetoric, and they taught young men whatever was necessary to keep their employers' families in power. Their strength was in their ability to "fill the buckets" of their students with a prescribed set of information established by the ruling class. By our measure, this information was painfully simple—basic number knowledge—algebra and geometry and higher maths, for example, were centuries away from being articulated. In any case, the sophists did seem to be experts at convincing people to believe their instructional services were worth a salary, and usually a fairly comfortable living arrangement.

Families hired these tutors to ensure that their sons would be able to pass the necessary tests (or win the necessary debates) required to hold positions in government, and as a result, keep the wealthy as the ruling class in Athens.

It may be argued that Sophists were a lot like many schools of today—public, private, charter, or choice. Social pressure encourages families to intentionally choose their school, rather than just attend the closest one to their home, and schools are obligated to sell themselves as "the best option" in order to maintain funding. While this may have begun as a strategy to increase school-wide and classroom effectiveness, there have been quite a lot of unintended consequences as well. While choice enrollment has driven improvement in many schools, the practice has also generated a fair amount of marketing—sometimes honest and sometimes not so much. The tax benefits for companies who create charter-school hedge funds is well documented (Strauss, 2014), but even in communities where rivaling high schools try to entice students to their halls, I have witnessed sometimes unscrupulous practices, from misrepresenting test data to exaggerating student engagement. In any case, like the rhetoric of the Sophists, some schools today garner their students based on their marketing plan and advertised test scores, which may or may not be a reflection of classroom practices or student efficacy as adults.

Socrates didn't believe in teaching for the sake of passing tests. More importantly, he believed in teaching his pupils to examine the world around them and to question everything. He wanted his students to vigorously pursue a definitive truth and to become the best version of themselves—what Aristotle would later coin as 'arete'. Although Socrates was portrayed in Aristophanes' play *The Clouds* as a sophist, other philosophers who knew Socrates, like Plato, and later Aristotle, argued that Socrates could never be considered a sophist. While he taught the art of argument, it was for the sake of uncovering truth. The sophists, on the other hand, taught argument as a method to win something—their arguments didn't rely on truth at all. Rather, their students were directed to know and employ a specific set of skills in order to win debate and rise to the top of societal structures.

Socrates changed the conversation of education from 'filling a bucket with skills and strategies' to 'nurturing student agency'—that is, he believed that education meant allowing the students to question and investigate their own interests and pursue their own personal truth.

It may be important to note here that he eventually perished by being forced to drink hemlock.

Before we too harshly judge those who sentenced him, we must consider how we might view him in our own time. Perhaps if he were teaching down the hall today, he wouldn't be thought of with the esteem that history has bestowed upon him. Consider this: how would his students perform on the state tests? Today, we rely so heavily on students knowing specific information for particular tests, we evaluate ("State Model Evaluation System", 2019) and establish pay for teachers on how well their students perform on them. (Teacher Compensation, 2021). And many would argue that this is sound practice. After all, how else might we determine an educator's effectiveness? Because their students were "good" or "curious" or "happy"? And if that were the case, how do we define those intangibles? What is "good"? How might we measure "curiosity"? What makes "happiness" (not in terms of elation, but in overall good/total fulfillment)?

Unlike those intangible goals, measuring student success by how well they can regurgitate information, or even practice skills they have been taught, is clean and easy. And while there is clearly a place for this amassing of knowledge and skills, education must endeavor to be more than that.

Based on the teachings of Socrates and, later, Plato and Aristotle, education is the essence of virtue, and the way one becomes virtuous is by seeking knowledge and gaining wisdom, not by mere achievement. In my mind, virtue is not attained by memorizing flashcards or designing a winning argument with material supplied by one's teacher. Therefore, the pedagogy of Socrates suggests that teachers who hope to produce virtuous students must plan for student voice and choice as they pursue their studies.

That "voice" and "choice" is at the heart of student agency—teachers must plan so that students have significant control over choices in their studies, and those choices must allow students to have meaningful influence on their life and community. No student should be expected (nor *encouraged*) to go through a school year and come out with simply a set of test scores to show what they have achieved. Instead, we must help them investigate what they can do that brings them a sense of better self-awareness and satisfaction and well-being. Perhaps eventually, we can help them consider what they can do in their community. What might they build or create that will have a lasting impact on the world around them?

This need not be a binary decision. Students should be able to have personal connection—choice in their studies—AND develop skills that help them achieve. But how do we do that in an environment that demands high achievement on high stakes tests? Well, at the very least, we must plan for it. Here is a suggested planning outline template for a 2-4 week study unit:

Unit Title

Content Objectives/Standards	Daily Warm Ups
	(editing, guided writing, free write, story problems, etc)
	Add Links Here
Social/Emotional/Management Objectives	Unit Lessons
	(direct instruction)
	Add Links Here
Objectives/Standards	Student Agency
	(choice in topic, product, process, assessment;ultimate challenge)
	Add Links Here
	Transitional and Review Games
Pre/Post Test (Add Links to Forms HERE and HERE)	Add Links Here

Intellectual property of ConstantlyTeach LLC©

Notice it includes links to 3 types of standards: academic, social emotional, and technology. It also includes links for teachers to store their self-made pre and posttests, daily warm-ups, direct instruction, agency, and games. If our teachers aren't planning for all these elements in their instruction, they must be given the tools to begin doing so immediately.

As you continue through this text, the types of links you'll want to put in each section of the unit planning outline will become more clear.

The important thing is to plan with the end in mind, build in opportunities for flexibility and adaptability, and consider the whole child (content objectives, social emotional objectives, technology objectives, social/emotional support, second language support, special needs modifications, and opportunities for play and agency) *before* the unit begins.

CHAPTER 4

The Peripatetic Journey
(Aristotle's Foundational Wisdom)

The next teacher we will examine is Aristotle. One of my favorite teacher strategies that Aristotle employed is 'peripatetic teaching', that is, he walked with his students as he taught them. (I've often wondered if Aristotle might have experienced overexcitabilities!)

Joking aside, he seemed to understand the mind—body connection of incorporating physical movement with thinking and learning. Although historical documents indicate that Aristotle didn't have anywhere close to 150 students a day (as most of our secondary teachers in the US do), I am constantly collecting tactics to incorporate this personal "walking and talking" practice into 21st century classrooms.

One strategy is to embed physical activity throughout the school day. John Ratey's book *Spark* explains in detail the many studies that have been conducted which connect exercise to brain function. One such study demonstrates that students who exercise at least 30 minutes a day (preferably in the morning) will learn vocabulary faster than other students (Ratey & Hagerman, 2008). A physical education teacher at one of the middle schools in my district took this research to heart and discovered time and again that the science holds true, even in an economically impacted community school. Beyond that, his school revised some of the school days throughout the year. During the usual four-minute passing periods, students were led through specific stretches or strategies for moving from one room to the next (walk with high knees, hop, etc). Of course, adaptations were made for students who couldn't participate, and appropriate grace and encouragement was made for students who *wouldn't* participate. The days were designed to explore the idea of fun and movement mixed with school. Beyond the passing period activities, teachers were encouraged to incorporate movement into their classes every day.

The most effective teachers I know make it a point to create classrooms in all content areas that work more as labs or workshops than 'sit and get' lectures, and, as much as is possible, build in physical movement to each class period. Problem based learning generally gets students moving within collaborative teams and manipulating materials as they think and troubleshoot solutions for engaging challenges. Extensive research (Terada, 2018) and the teachers I worked with discovered that building in a few 3-minute movement breaks (or even better—dance breaks!) to be an effective practice for keeping students engaged and energized for learning and creating—even during the challenging times of Covid and remote learning.

While many of these strategies happen sometimes in elementary school, and sporadically in middle school, my experience showed that they all but disappear in many high school classrooms. For many teachers, the stress of high stakes assessment has created a metaphorical, internal tug of war between what they want to do and what they think they are supposed to do in their classrooms, because they think school can only be one or the other—a place of joy or a place of learning. From my perspective, it is the refusal to incorporate fun and activity into the classroom that is diminishing learning. And Aristotle knew this over 2000 years ago. Stop and consider now—how can you build movement into your daily sessions in order to foster deeper thinking? While chapter 8 of this book will have more ideas for games and movement, here are a few suggestions:

Activity	The Gist
Gallery Walks	Students walk to different areas of the room to access posted resources—they discuss the resources with other students who are moving with them
Speed Dating	Students line up in opposite rows and discuss a specific question for 2 minutes before moving one step to the right and speaking to the next person across from them. (Students slide into the other row when they reach the end of the line)
Musical Mingle	Students move around the room to entertaining music. When the music stops, they must find a thought partner to discuss an idea or even to work with for an entire activity.
Polarity Polls	Opposite spectrums are posted across the room and students line themselves up based on their position on a particular prompt.
Socratic Soccer	Keep a soccer ball handy that you have written some standing prompts on—such as "predict what will be the outcome" or "compare this situation/equation to another" or "explain an alternate approach". Have the students stand and toss the ball to one another—the catcher responds to the question where his/her right thumb lands.
Find it!	For online classes that need a short break from screen time: Ask students to take 5-10 minutes to search for something in their house that represents a specific idea (i.e. 'find something that demonstrates how form follows function—or not'). When they return, they can work in breakout groups to show and explain their findings. (Remind the students to take a bathroom and snack break in this window as well!)

Perhaps more significantly than his idea of learning-while-in-action though, Aristotle developed the practice of naming some very important skills. Specifically, he named the three appeals of rhetoric: ethos, pathos, and logos. Further, he required that his students create a balance of all three appeals in each of their arguments.

He also established the laws of logic which are the foundation not only for truthful argument but also for algebra and the scientific method, which would follow hundreds of years later.

What a wonderful concept to teach to our students: Once we affix names to things, we can teach them and discuss them and ultimately revise them (hopefully as an improvement). Whenever I led a unit with this idea, the vocabulary portion of study became easier because it was more meaningful to the students.

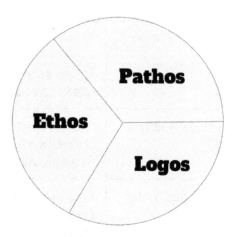

As I reflect on Aristotle's influence on me as an educator, I am drawn to his recognition of the need to balance our lives, first our mind and body, and also our thinking, with the appeals. If we cannot instill a guideline for creating sound arguments, which would be ideal, I would hope that we can at least teach about these three appeals so that our students are critical consumers of the rhetoric that surrounds and imposes itself on them. Students as well as adults are bombarded daily with advertising, political campaigns, and multi-media which are designed with the intention of manipulating unaware audiences. Developing the skills to recognize ethos, pathos, and logos will allow young and old alike to dodge unscrupulous tactics and objectives of commercial ne'er-do-wells.

Finally, Aristotle established the idea that skills, concepts, and facts must be named to be discussed.

Sometimes when I talk with teachers about the importance of allowing choice for their students, they interpret this to mean that the students don't need to learn content. While I will (and do!) argue that we aren't in the business of "filling buckets" or making our students memorize and regurgitate facts and stats, I still recognize the value of presenting and discussing important constructs of whatever discipline one teaches. Without common vocabulary, people who work within any field cannot effectively communicate to create or improve that field. There is no question that any field of work has a set of vocabulary and strategies and philosophy that its experts use. Students need to learn this concept so that they may one day converse with others who share their same interests and passions.

For example, as an English teacher, I will always help my students understand the mechanics of writing by playing with sentences every day. In my mind, students should be able to understand how phrases and clauses are used as modifiers so they may appropriately revise when a sentence isn't clear in its meaning. Additionally, though I didn't drill and skill them on logical fallacies, I did introduce them to a list of those fallacies, and we often played games to find them in literary and non-fiction articles or commercials or Twitter posts. And the success indicators I used in my class, even when they were student developed, articulated the effective use of such skills for high achievement. Evolution of thought requires a certain familiarity with what has come before in order to fine tune it or break away from it completely in moving forward. Therefore, it is imperative that teachers help students find common vocabulary and other foundations for discussing any area of thought.

My take-away from Aristotle is depicted below—I kept some version of it on the wall in my classroom as a point of reference for students to consider in their reading, writing, and discussions. As we learned about any topic, students were also exploring this Aristotelian wisdom and applying it to their modern-day learning.

The Wisdom of Aristotle

Balance of Body, Mind, & Communication	Balance of Appeals (Ethos, Pathos, Logos)
Respect for Logic (Avoid logical fallacies!)	Common Knowledge for Meaningful Discussions (Are we using the vernacular of the experts?)

In an effort to consistently visit those ideals in my own classroom, let's take a look at a tool I've created to guide myself and other teachers through the process of designing an instructional unit. It is designed to be copied for any unit and then modified with appropriate images, articles, rubrics, and assessments.

This next segment will walk you through the different slide styles on the template. Take some time to consider a specific unit and how you might use this tool to help organize a plan to help your students' learning.

The Lesson Planning Template

Let's work with the understanding that there are 10 basic slide templates. You can easily replicate them on Microsoft Presentation© or Google Slides©. Although I recommend keeping the order of the first five slides, you have the agency to organize and modify them as best suits you and your classroom needs. The slides templates are:

Cover Slide
1. Enduring Learning
2. Unit Goals
3. Final Assignment
4. Sample product
5. Collaboratively designed Rubric
6. Mini Lesson
7. Learning Exploration
8. Daily Goal
9. Daily Reflection

Slide 1—Cover Slide

The cover slide is the students' first encounter with the unit. Replace the image there with your own thematic image, keeping in mind that pictures can help students connect to material they are learning and jog their memory to access that material later. Seeing the picture on your classroom website will also help students access the unit easily. This particular slide was for a unit on narrative writing for 7th and 8th graders. The unit was called "Picture This", and each student created a photo book with pictures and text about a topic of specific interest to them.

In your own classroom, you will learn to know your students and can customize the images best—something both familiar to them and connected to their new learning. In any case, this cover slide is your opportunity to "brand" your study unit.

Notice there is a place at the bottom left of this slide to embed a pre-test. We will talk about that later in this chapter. For now, keep in mind that it is a best practice to give the students the pre-test before diving in further to the unit.

Slides 2-4

The next three slides are even more important to setting the stage in your classroom for students to be ready to explore new ideas. They are "Enduring Learning"; "Learning Goals"; and "Final Assignment".

"The Enduring Learning" slide will state up to five long term objectives for your students—what will they learn in this unit that you would like them to remember 40 years from now? These are all connected directly to district standards, but I prefer to use "kid speak" for my slide shows. Here are the sample slides from a short narrative writing unit I taught:

Slide 2

Enduring Learning	You can create a book!! (Lots of them!)
	Books are created as expressions from authors and designed with an audience in mind
	Artists are 'great manipulators'

The Enduring Learning is followed by the short-term learning goals. Considering local and national standards, create a list of up to six immediate skill goals you have for your students. Then, allow the students to use that (and their own imagination) to narrow the list and select a total of 4 goals, personally aligned to their needs.

For example, below is a list of the goals that I suggested for the "Picture This" unit:

Slide 3

Learning Goals Menu (Students must list four of their own goals—at least two must come from this list.)	• I can use and show others how to use basic iPad or phone camera tools • I can define and apply the design-inspired 'Rule of Thirds" • I can list and employ multiple narrative techniques such as dialogue, description, pacing, reflection, and plot to develop rich, interesting experiences, events, and/or characters as I create a picture book • I can develop a word bank for a selected topic, share working definitions of the terms in the list, and integrate the words effectively into my writing • I can access and use photo editing tools for effect • I can integrate poetic devices as well as figurative and sensory language to capture the action and convey experiences and events.

Here are the learning goal lists generated by three different students in that class:

Angelica's Learning Goals for "Picture This"	At the end of the unit, I will be able to: • Define and apply the design 'Rule of Thirds" • Develop a word bank for a selected topic, share working definitions of the terms in the list, and integrate the words effectively into my writing • Know and explain the habitat, diet, and common behaviors of the magpie. • Include and punctuate dialogue in a story effectively.

	At the end of the unit, I will be able to:
Harrison's Learning Goals for "Picture This"	• Use and show others how to use basic iPad or phone camera tools • Access and use photo editing tools for effect • List and employ multiple narrative techniques such as dialogue, description, pacing, reflection, and plot to develop rich, interesting experiences, events, and/or characters as I create a picture book access and use photo editing tools for effect • Learn and share a history and 3 "tricks" of skateboarding

	At the end of the unit, I will be able to:
Riley's Learning Goals for "Picture This"	• Define and apply the design 'Rule of Thirds" • Develop a word bank for a selected topic, share working definitions of the terms in the list, and integrate the words effectively into my writing • Access and use photo editing tools for effect • Integrate poetic devices as well as figurative and sensory language to capture the action and convey experiences and events.

As you can see, Angelica chose two of the learning goals from my list and two of her own; Harrison chose three of the goals from my list and one of his own, and Riley selected all his goals from the list I provided. This autonomy allows them to dial down to what truly interests them and continue to foster a love of learning. In the end, most of my students were able to perform successfully on summative assessments that covered all the original goals I listed, even though they preferred to focus on only some of them.

I usually add a second slide of learning goals that focus specifically on social emotional learning (I like to think of SEL as "soft but essential learning"). I generally include a list of three skills about which I will provide direct instruction (via mini lessons). As they did with the academic learning goals, students narrow the list—in this case they select only one of the skills to focus on during a unit. For example, my SEL goals for this book unit were:

Soft and Essential Learning Goals (Your teacher will provide lessons on each of these—choose ONE that you will focus on during this unit)	• I will learn and practice strategies for self-advocacy • I will learn and practice strategies for perseverance • I will learn and practice skills to be more flexible in thinking and/or responding to change

Beyond the direct instruction, this SEL goal is revisited regularly through student reflection during the study unit.

Slide 4 in the template shows the cumulative assignment.

Slide 4

Assignment:	In this unit, you will use an iPad or your phone to take a series of photographs. You will then use those photos to inspire an original, narrative text. Then, you will digitally design a 20 page book which will be printed and delivered to your home. (Or another product of your choice after you talk it over with your teacher). It is important that your final product includes all the "key" parts of a published text (cover, title page with publication info, etc.), and that you employ multiple narrative techniques such as dialogue, description, pacing, reflection, and plot to develop rich, interesting experiences, events, and/or characters as you create a picture book.

When using this template, it is important to fill in the enduring learning, the learning goals, and the end assignment and share all that information with the students *from the beginning of the unit.* The reason for this is because many gifted students thrive on knowing the "whys" of their instruction. Simon Sinek depicts the importance of "the why" in his Golden Circle Model, which he applies to business. He explains that while knowing "what to do" and "how to do it" is obviously necessary to success, our motivation comes from understanding "why" we do it. (Sinek, 2013). In the classroom, if the only "why" is a test, the whole thing feels pointless. Gifted students in particular, seem to *need* to feel that their learning will result in intellectual or creative expansion.

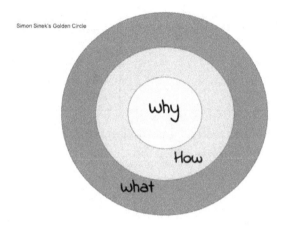

Simon Sinek's Golden Circle

If the outcome of your study unit is a specific product, do your best to allow for flexibility and student input if they suggest something different. For example, if you want the student to design a city in a geometry class, but he would prefer to design an amusement park, try to be open to that.

One time in my own classroom, I was teaching a unit that culminated in a particular digital platform—because it was a platform I knew how to use and could instruct the students how to use it. When a few of the students said they had used that platform in other classes and they wanted to do something different, I panicked. I didn't know how to use the platform they were requesting. How could I ask them to make a product that I didn't understand how to use myself?

After talking it over with another colleague though, I realized that I don't have to know how to use every software created for the students to have access to it. The beauty of the internet is that it is a treasure trove of tools and instruction—and the sooner we can help students learn this, the better!

Also, as a result of their investigations, I learned new platforms for creating digital products. It was absolutely a win-win.

◇◇◇

As demonstrated in the tutorial information embedded in the template, I now offer students the following caveat when creating a product-based assessment: *"or another tool/product of your choice after you speak with your teacher about it."*

Ultimately, what they are learning reaches far beyond the product they create. The important learning is outlined in the goals, highlighted in the assignment, and articulated in the rubric. The platform they use is really to increase their engagement, plus it teaches them to be self-directed learners.

Slide 5 in the template gives the students a link to the assignment's rubric. Here is the final rubric that my students and I developed together for the narrative unit:

Slide 5

Δ (Delta/Suggested Changes)	**Picture This Book Rubric**	**+** (Plus/Strengths)
	Digital Product • Book is colorful, neat, and attractive suggesting an advanced level of workmanship. • Text fonts are appropriate for the content and carry a theme • Images and words are clear and large enough for viewers to observe • Technology is used effectively • Final text is 20 pages total	
	Content/Organization • Eye catching cover hints at content • Title page includes title/author/publishing date	

	Writing	
	• Establishes a situation, one or more points of view, and introduces a narrator and/or characters • Employs multiple narrative techniques such as dialogue, description, pacing, reflection, and plot to develop rich, interesting experiences, events, and/or characters • Uses a variety of techniques consistently to sequence events that build on one another • Uses precise words and phrases, details, and sensory language consistently to convey a vivid picture of the events • Provides a satisfying conclusion based on previous events • Integrates ideas and details from source material effectively • Has very few or no errors in usage and/or conventions that interfere with meaning	

It is valuable for you to consider the learning outcomes you are working toward and make a rubric that is unique for each unit. You are encouraged to use whatever style of rubric suits you best, though I enjoy the freedom that the single-column rubric gives.

Also, and more importantly, I give my draft of the rubric to my students and have them workshop a final scoring guide as a class. This action alone is a great builder of agency, as it sends a clear message to the students that their ideas are important and valid. It also helps the students clearly define what they are working toward creating, solving, and learning over the course of the unit.

Pre- and Post-Tests

In terms of building a sense of agency with the students, the pre and post-test links are also incredibly important. Allowing them the exposure to what the summative test will cover gives them the control over knowing what to study. I have found over the years that my data is most valuable when I create the pre and post-tests at the same time—with this practice, I am confident that I will test the same skills on both tests— and they are the skills that I intended to teach during the unit. Also, as noted earlier, it's most efficient to dive directly into the pre-test data as quickly as possible and before beginning the unit. You may find that you have underestimated your students' skill abilities when creating the unit.

A few years ago, I was working with a young teacher who called me around 8:30 at night with terror in her voice.

"I just went over the pre-tests," she said, on the verge of tears.

"What happened?" I asked, trying to guess what could have her so shaken.

"They aced it. The lowest score in the class was 85%. What do I do?"

Honestly, as much as I knew this teacher and I would now have a lot of work to do in a short amount of time, I was relieved. I had been asked to work with her because this group of gifted students (and their parents) had been complaining that the class was 'boring.' The teacher was adhering to the district-designed curriculum with fidelity, and she was confused about how to make things more interesting.

Prior to working with me, she had not been using pre-test data. But now, she could see clearly that it wasn't *her* that was boring…she was rehashing things they already knew. She, like so many teachers, was doing her job and following the curriculum. The problem was, this group of students already had a good grasp of the ideas (vocabulary, reading skills, etc.) that the curriculum prescribed. That is because a good curriculum, such as what my district has developed, is designed to spiral up, which means that many concepts are revisited over the years—that is how most people learn. Gifted students, however, generally learn things much more quickly. They don't need to go over and over an idea to understand how to use it. They needed more challenge—an opportunity to learn more difficult material as well as create something new and unique with it.

As a response, we did not throw out the unit, which was focused on historical fiction. Instead, we adjusted the learning goals and revised the pre-test, using significantly more difficult reading material and exploring more complex literary concepts. For example, instead of using a passage from *Amelia's War* by Ann Rinaldi to ask students to identify a foil, we used a passage from *The Red Badge of Courage* by Stephen Crane and asked them to identify juxtaposition. Crane's text is not only more complex in content, but was also written in the 19th century, bringing in a new level of language complexity and testing the skills required to navigate that. While 'foil' is a term used when contrasting one character with one other character, 'juxtaposition' is more complicated and contrasts not only characters but also places or concepts. (Also, juxtaposition has four more syllables than foil, which makes it a far more appealing word to a seventh-grade gifted student.)

We likewise adjusted the instructional pieces (mini lessons) throughout the unit to address the richer vocabulary, devices, and writing styles.

Since students were selecting their own historical texts for their literature circles, we didn't need to change the reading options—only the instructional pieces which we would use in "mini-lessons" along the way. We already knew to provide higher level reading material for this class, but even if they were reading a book marked as grades 4-7, they would likely be able to address richer devices (like juxtaposition). If a similar issue had occurred in a math course, we might have replaced a question about simple multiplication with a question about exponents. It all depends on the learning goals and the next logical step of such a skill set.

The beauty of the pre-test and post-test is that it assures us we are building on what the students already know rather than recycling or repeating it. It also allows students (and parents, administrators, and you, the teacher) to have a baseline for determining the growth students make over the course of the instructional unit. It gives everyone data to determine the benefits of their work.

Mini Lesson and Learning Exploration Slides

Mini Lesson	Link to a 5–10-minute direct instruction lesson—you will likely have a mini lesson each day of the unit or several days a week.
	These lessons will align with your learning goals (for example, this is where I added a lesson on point of view—1st, 2nd, and 3rd person narrators)

Mini lessons should be designed to target the skills that pre-test data indicated as the greatest student need. They shouldn't last more than 5-10 minutes of a class period, and they should use a balance of accessibility and challenge.

Learning exploration allows students more independence as they explore teacher-supplied articles and videos. This is also a space where students can locate credible sources of their own to share with their classmates. A number of teachers I worked with used this slide for flipped classrooms or for non-contact days during the Covid pandemic.

	Attach readings here and instruct students to
Learning Exploration	• Read the articles or view the videos provided • Annotate with questions and noticings • Discuss the articles/annotations with your group (As the facilitator, provide time to discuss and to seek further resources when applicable)

Daily Goals and Daily Reflection Slides

Another benefit of this unit template is the built-in points of student independence. As you scroll through the template, you'll see that every day includes an invitation for students (Daily Goals) to set a "to-do" list for themselves as they dive into their work. This may be something they want to learn, do, or create for the day. It is also a good place for students to consider organizational goals or emotional regulation goals for a day.

The reflection slide can be a place for students to collect notes to themselves, informal formative assessment for their teachers, or notes either during class or as self-assigned homework if they can't get the job done in the class time allotted. This can also be a cue to occasionally review their semester and unit goals and consider how they align with their daily work.

The Lesson Template is designed with "the wisdom of Aristotle" in mind—it respects logic as it keeps the teacher and the students on a schedule to move seamlessly through a unit. Allowing teachers to save the work for another year (with appropriate revisions as they are needed) provides at least a little balance in the lives of teachers and students—teachers who can streamline lesson planning and students who can easily access the work and information they need for learning.

It includes slides that appeal to meaningful discussion, personal reflection, and direct instruction. (Ethos, pathos, logos). Also, students will be accumulating common knowledge as well as pursuing their unique interests—a marriage of curriculum and autonomy.

A final bonus is that this template allows students to work from home in a hybrid model as easily as they can in a classroom setting.

All these elements combine to provide a healthy and personal approach to learning and student agency.

CHAPTER 5

Building on the Familiar
(Utilizing Anne Sullivan's Realization)

Although my own parents did not have much in the way of formal schooling, both of my grandmothers liked to remind me that "teaching is in my blood."

Before she met my grandfather, my paternal grandmother, who was born in 1904, became a prairie schoolteacher in Nebraska at the age of 19 (having a high school diploma was qualification enough to teach K-12 in the early 20th century). Once married of course, teaching (beyond her own children), was out of the question, as married women were prohibited from holding such a job in 1927. In other words, hers was a rather short-lived career.

There were two other important teacher-role models in my family as well. My maternal grandfather's sister (Great Aunt Thelma) never had children and was able to teach for about 30 years in Oakland, California—from the 1930s into the 1970s. When I decided to go into teaching myself in the 1980s, she wrote a scant couple of letters and sent me one of her college texts. She died when I was a very new teacher; we weren't close, and my mother found her to be very rigid, as I recall, but I read the seemingly ancient text she sent me with the furious hope of finding some bit of insight as I navigated my first few years of teaching. In the years since, I have sadly lost track of it—though I am certain it is somewhere in a box in storage! In any case, I could not locate it to offer it legitimate citation here. Still, it merits some description here.

It was an ancient little book—long out of print even back in the 1980s—and I remember imagining the narrator to be holding a teacup, pinky extended, and sounding at least a little bit proper, like Aunt Thelma. It included a few instructional tips that I have held on to—such as (and I am paraphrasing from memory):

○ *One must never allow the frivolity of current gossip or Hollywood news to be discussed in the classroom.*

○ *Always make the classroom a place of exploration in the skills of an intellect.*

However, I have chosen to ignore—or rather, disregard—other ideas presented by the text. For example, it also (as I recall) discussed the importance of learning everything step-by-step—

○ *Do not let the student believe that he can approach one skill before he has mastered its prerequisite*—an idea I thought, when I read it in the 1980s, was off-kilter.

Certainly, it helps to learn addition before multiplication, or scriptwriting before movie making...but no law of nature says there is only one way to learn how to do something. I've known plenty of students, for example, who have made YouTube© or TikTok© videos without ever writing a script or making a storyboard, and some who built forts in their yard without blueprints. Of course, their products had room for improvement, but what creation doesn't? The immersion into such an undertaking was led by curiosity, and it fostered a love of learning and problem solving and testing of new ideas and learning some more.

There was, though, something that rang very true from that book—even so much that I took it on as a regular part of my classroom regime—and that was the idea of the student exhibition.

The Student Exhibition

According to Aunt Thelma's book, every student, at least one time per year, must have an opportunity to demonstrate what they've learned and then present it to an authentic audience. That audience could be a group of students, if necessary, but would better be extended, it suggested, to a local business or rancher or farmer, an agricultural club, a library staff, or a doctor. Whatever the idea was that the student had pursued through research, writing, and/or design, it said, should be shared with someone who can offer valuable feedback. And though it was incongruent with the "step-by-step" advice the book had purported earlier, I thought it would also be good if the chosen audience could perhaps learn something new from the student as well. As a new teacher (and now, after more than 30 years in a classroom) the idea of this had many, many layers of value in my mind.

I cannot emphasize enough the power I have seen from students working to produce something for a "real" audience. Sometimes their classroom peers feel real enough, but often, they need more—especially if they are exceptionally good at something. That is why, as an educator, I was so often drawn to student-produced plays and newspapers and yearbooks. When students realize they are creating a product that will be consumed by someone they want to impress (for whatever reason), they will put so much more time and intellectual effort into it.

This idea can come to fruition in many ways, but however it occurs, it will have the greatest meaning and value to students if the work grows out of an organic, personal interest. Furthermore, if we recognize the skills dictated by our curricula as tools to help students excel, this sort of personalized approach to learning will be the necessary catalyst to help them learn deeply and with enthusiasm.

That personalized approach to an enthusiastic pursuit of deep learning connects us to the star of this chapter. One memorable book from my childhood was a picture book about Helen Keller and Anne Sullivan. I don't know how I acquired this book—though it likely belonged to one of my older sisters—but I just loved it. I loved the artist's drawing of the pretty blue dress with petticoats that Helen wore, and I loved the dark spectacles drawn on the face of Anne Sullivan.

When I was a little girl, Laura Ingalls Wilder and Anne Sullivan were the first teachers I remember reading about, and, perhaps because I envisioned them as my own grandmother, teaching on the prairie, they influenced me tremendously.

If you don't know her story, Anne Sullivan was the teacher of Helen Keller. Keller was rendered blind and deaf at a very early age due to fever. By the age of seven, she had become uncontrollable, and her parents were at a loss as to what to do with her. They couldn't keep her or the rest of the family safe at home unless she learned some way to interact with her world.

Enter Anne Sullivan: Anne was born to poor immigrants in the 1860s. After contracting a debilitating illness at the age of 5, she was rendered blind, and when she was 8, her mother died of tuberculosis. Feeling helpless or overwhelmed, her father abandoned Anne and her brother to the Tewksbury Almshouse for orphans. Sadly, her brother died shortly after their arrival, but Anne stayed at Tewksbury until 1880, when she went on to study at the Perkins School for the Blind. Though she had never been to school before and also had little direction in the way of social graces, Anne managed to work hard and excel at Perkins. She said later in life that she never felt as though she truly fit in there; nonetheless, she went on to become the valedictorian of her class. As a result, when the Keller family wrote to the director of the Perkins school, Anne Sullivan was the first tutor he recommended to help the family with their child, Helen.

After a bout with an illness and subsequent fever (perhaps scarlet fever or meningitis, but it is unclear), 19-month-old Helen had lost her ability to both see and hear. Consequently, she also lost access to the sounds that would have helped her learn to speak. For nearly five of her first six years of life, Helen was living in a dark and silent world, unable to communicate her needs clearly to anyone. When Anne Sullivan arrived at the Keller's home in 1886, all of that was to change in profound and historic ways.

There is so much I love about Anne Sullivan, and I invite you to read about her and Helen Keller, but here's what resonates most for me:

"Start with what they know."

In 1962, the story was famously made into a movie starring Anne Bancroft and Patty Duke. The iconic scene in the film is when Sullivan finally breaks through to Helen's dark, quiet world. She has spent weeks, months, diligently signing letters and word symbols into little Helen Keller's hands, but one day, when they are out getting water, she decides to try something different. She puts Helen's hand into the water and then signs the symbol for water into her hand...and finally Helen has an epiphany. For the first time, she understands that all this crazy movement of fingers in her palm was intended to communicate. Once she makes that connection, the world opens up! Under the tutelage of Anne Sullivan, Helen goes on to learn American

Sign Language and read Braille, as well as finish both primary and secondary schooling, graduate with a Bachelor of Arts from Radcliffe College, write multiple books and become a political activist, and be welcomed into the White House by every president from Grover Cleveland to Lyndon Johnson. But all of that began because Anne Sullivan understood the value of putting symbols to something that little Helen already knew—water.

The take-away from Anne Sullivan is that **students learn more and faster when we start with the familiar.** Madeline Hunter echoed that with the anticipatory set in her Master Teaching Design, (Hunter & Hunter, 2004) but let's take it beyond that.

Remember that our gifted students think differently than about 95% of their peers. Common resistance refrains are "how will I ever use this?" or "what does this have to do with me?" Hunter's anticipatory set tries to establish a common story for the whole class and thereby "hook" them into engagement. The anticipatory set is a very good beginning to "starting where they are", but in order for your most gifted students to stay connected, the guided practice that follows will need to allow for diverse options that align with individual curiosity.

For example, a curriculum may dictate that students know how to make and use a spreadsheet to organize data, and let's say that a 9th grade teacher wisely ties this skill to a writing unit for consumer product review. Under Hunter's model, the teacher may give the students a particular product to review and then provide the students with several articles about various brands of that product, such as car wax. Then, the students would set up a table or spreadsheet to track specific qualities of the different brands. Following is a sample of the spreadsheet created by a student for this assignment:

Criteria Table

Criteria	RainX 16.9 oz bottle	Turtle Wax 16 oz bottle	Walbernize 32 oz bottle
Price	$8.37	$11.15	$13.99
Does it protect (on a scale from 1-10) *	9.5	10	10
Is it easy (on a scale from 1-10)	9.5	6	10
Is it messy (Backwards)	7	9	10
Does it clean? (on a scale from 1-10)	9	8	9.5
Total points (Out of 40)	35	33	39.5

* 1 being "not at all"; 5 being "it's okay"; and 10 being "absolutely wonderful".

While learning in this manner (skill first, activity later) works for many students, it doesn't work for all of them. A student who is taught this way may learn the concept but not the value of a skill. (Or he may not learn the skill at all.) If the student finds no value in the skill, she is unlikely to use the skill later or remember it long term. So, when instructional delivery like this doesn't work, we must help the struggling student to find something familiar and personally meaningful and interesting so that they can learn the value of the tools they are given. Otherwise, the information or skills being taught may never take hold.

What do we do next? Educator and author, Carol Ann Tomlinson, points us in the right direction with differentiation. (Tomlinson, 2018) Many of my colleagues dutifully offered leveled readings or assignments in three different categories to accommodate diverse learning needs, and some were brave enough to extend even beyond that. In my experience, our gifted students thrived when their teachers were flexible enough to allow *individualized* choice in topic, product, process, or assessment.

If your curriculum dictates that you must teach students how to use a table or spreadsheet or conduct a consumer product review, ask them to learn the skills by applying them to *something that matters to them*. Almost every student has a "dream item" he would like to purchase, whether it be a pair of shoes, a summer "fun pass" to a local amusement park, or a dream car—or maybe even the college of their choice. Here is a clip from a spreadsheet made by a student who created the spreadsheet for his college search:

CA	Priority	College Name	Early action/Priç Regular Admissi	Majors	Cost	Years of World Langu	Strong In	Athletics/Baseba	Application Fee	Percent Students Un	Admissions	Common App?
		University of Manchester	6/30 for Internat N/A	Aerospace Engin	£9,445 or $12,25 N/A		Aerospace Engineerin N/A		$78.02-£50.00	72%	Scores of 4 on 3 AP te	Yes
		CSU	12/17	2/1	Mathematics/BA	$25,424-$27,300 2	Science	D1	$50	29%	https://admissions.co	Yes
		CU Boulder	11/15	1/15/19	Aerospace Engin	$27,884	3	Engineering	D1	$50	29%	MAPS? https://www.i	Yes
		Embry-Riddle Aeronautical Univ	2/15	N/A	Multiple Aerosp	$17,000	N/A	Aerospace Engineerin	D2	$50	16%	2 Letters of Recomm	No
		Kansas State	11/1	N/A	Aerospace Mino	$17,000	2	General	D1	$40	27%	Must Print and Mail N	No
		Massachusetts Institute of Tech	11/1	1/1	Aerospace prog	$23,000	2	Engineering	D3	$75	94%	https://mitadmission	No
		Rensselaer Polytechnic Institute	11/1, 12/15	1/15	Aerospace Engin	$35,000	0 required	Engineering	D3	$70	57%	Required Lab Based P	Yes
		University of Kansas	11/1	7/15	Aerospace Engin	$19,000	2	Engineering and other	D1	$40	25%	Need ACT https://adn	Yes
		CU Denver			Astrophysics/MW	$7,336		Graduate School Mostly		$35		N/A	
		DU			Astrophysics/MW	$63,000		Not strong in Degree's interested in		$65		N/A	
		Maine			Chemistry/BA/BI	$13,476.34		Not strong in Degree's interested in		$25		N/A	
		Stevens Institute of Technology			Multiple Engine	$18,050		Technology		$75		N/A	
		UCCS			Mechanical Engi	$29,741		Engineering and others		$50		N/A	
		UNC			Aerospace/Air fc	$8,978.20		Cultural Education		$45		N/A	
		Arizona State University	11/1	7/28	Multiple Aerosp	$45,836 (without vid)		Engineering		$70	21%	N/A	Yes
		Case Western Reserve Universit	11/1, 1/15	1/15	Aerospace Engin	$28,000		Engineering		$70	70%	N/A	Yes
		Clarkson University	12/1	1/15	Aeronautical Eng	$29,000		Research		$50	81%	N/A	Yes
		Illinois Tech	12/1	7/28	Aerospace Engin	$18,500		Technology		N/A	68%	N/A	Yes
		Mississippi State Bagwell School	7/28	N/A	Aerospace Engin	$16,410 (general)		Engineering		$40	23%	N/A	Yes
		Montana State University	N/A	3/1	Aerospace Mino	$17,000		General		$30	28%	N/A	No

Rather than starting with "how to make a spreadsheet", the teacher in this case allowed his students to begin instead with collecting the data. Then, when they were having trouble sorting out the information, he introduced the magic of the table or spreadsheet and how easily it would allow them to organize and sort and even graph the information they had gathered. Many gifted students benefit from this kind of learning—gathering information and then discovering a tool to manipulate it and use it more effectively. Conversely, many gifted students will have found *a better way than your spreadsheet* to organize the information they have gathered. The challenge then becomes, can you be flexible and adaptable enough to incorporate their new thinking into your lesson?

In my own classroom and in working with many teachers, I have observed that it is this kind of approach to learning and creating that engages students—especially gifted students—the most effectively. This is as true for adults as it is for young people. When an adult is learning how to use her new cell phone, for instance, she rarely sits down and reads the entire manual first. Instead, she attempts to do something and then learns how to use particular functions or apps as she needs to use them. Yet, we so often ask students to learn a particular skill without any context—or with a context that may be removed from their impression of importance. When we allow them the choice to learn about something that truly interests them personally, they find a need for tools that will further their study—and then we can provide them! As they are pursuing a meaningful expansion of thinking for themselves, they will be learning how to use tools of the trade and strategies of the experts, all while creating something that will be a source of pride for themselves.

This brings us back to the text from my Great Aunt Thelma and the student exhibition: How can we utilize the student exhibition to support learning in a way that is meaningful and thereby engaging to our learners?

It turns out, there are many, many possibilities.

School-wide, club-specific conferences and contests:
Technology Student Association©, Decca©, International Thespian Conference© (Thes-con), Math Counts©, Trivia Bowl©, Destination Imagination©, VEX Robotics©, etc.

School-wide performances and events:
Plays, sports, concerts, cultural fairs, science fairs, learning expos, etc.

School-wide publications
Yearbook, newspaper, student handbook, orientation videos, etc.

We can easily move beyond the school community into district, state, national, and even international forums for our gifted students to extend their learning risks, their creations, and the understanding of their place in the bigger world.

Other personalized projects for your students to explore are contests and scholarship opportunities. There are many scholarship programs throughout the country starting as early as 6th grade. Are these being announced and supported with work time toward them within specific classrooms and schools—or do we just expect students to seek out such opportunities for themselves on their own time? True, these contests are easily discovered with quick internet searches, and scholarship opportunities are generally available through the school counseling center, but I have found that many students are unaware that they should even be looking. Perhaps we would be providing more equitable access to such prospects if we were bringing those extensions into our classrooms and offering incentive to complete them as an alternate assignment or extension. Such a practice would connect students to authentic audiences for their personal interests and support them with the gift of time and attention to complete and submit these opportunities—which would be more valuable to a student who has already mastered the personal narrative or another performance indicator in a prescribed syllabus. Connecting students to the communities provided by these fellowships would most certainly be lighting a fire under them—igniting their enthusiasm for putting one foot in front of the other and moving steadily toward a future in which they have a creative hand.

Once we realize that our student's personal interests will drive them ever forward on the path of curiosity, we can recognize that the only tools we truly need to give them are those predicted some four decades ago by author John Naisbitt, in his first edition of *Megatrends*. "*In a world that is constantly changing, there is no one subject or set of subjects that will serve you for the foreseeable future, let alone for the rest of your life. The most important skill to acquire now is learning how to learn.*" (Naisbitt, 1982) In other words, students must learn the strategies for accessing information and those skills that help them distinguish between credible and non-credible sources (the evolution of Aristotle!).

Our gifted students are not interested in simply learning what has come before them—nor should they be. Furthermore, when we come to them always with the intention of "having something to teach them" —especially if it is about work ethic or attitude—we are coming from a place that is privileged and oppressive. It is not an older generation's job to put thoughts into young people's minds and then expect them to stay stuck there. Rather, it is the job of a true educator to help students develop the personal confidence and acumen to tap into their own imagination and then pursue and access the information they need to build *their* vision of a new world. We can do this most effectively when we start with what feels familiar to them and then encourage them to take flight. Beyond that, and to extend the metaphor, once they take flight, we must be willing to flex and adapt when it takes them in a new and even unfamiliar direction. Once they start down the path of innovation, our question must become, "what can we learn from them?"

CHAPTER 6

Discovering Hidden Gifts
(Moving beyond 'Dangerous Minds')

I have paired the next two teachers together, mostly because I see them in the realm of my contemporary influences. That is, they are not just from my history books—they were practicing their craft in the early part of my teacher education and career. And to me, they also represent the importance of breaking down some of the social constructs that existed more invisibly in the 1970s and 80s.

This is not to say that the stories of these two teachers and their students changed the dynamics of racial or inner-city inequality in our country. In fact, in many ways, both movies that resulted from their life-experiences (*Stand and Deliver*© and *Dangerous Minds*©) *perpetuated* the unfair stereotype of inner-city students—especially those of color—being chronic underachievers. So, to clarify, that is not why I'm lifting these two teachers. Rather, in the spirit of high-lighting positive contributions, I have included them to demonstrate how they helped me be a better teacher. Here are their stories and what they meant to me:

Jaime Escalante was arguably the most famous teacher in the United States in the 1980s and 90s. Born in La Paz, Bolivia, Escalante taught math and physics at Bolivian schools for nearly ten years before coming to the United States to attain a better life for his family. Once in the US, he began work as a janitor in a diner while he learned English. He eventually earned a degree in math and physics, as well as a teaching credential from Cal State University, Los Angeles. He rose to fame as a result of his work from 1974 to 1982, when he held a teaching position at Garfield High School, in Pasadena, CA. The school, in a heavily Latinx community, had a reputation of serving troubled students and also of being on academic watch: it was in danger of losing its accreditation.

While teaching at Garfield, Escalante identified a number of students who were viewed as "unteachable" by his colleagues and recruited them into a math path that culminated in an AP Calculus course.

At Escalante's inducing, these students studied before and after school and on weekends. He visited their families, some who were not supportive because they needed their children to earn extra income for the family. He dissuaded some from spending so much time in band or athletics so they could exceed in math instead—a path, he knew, which would take them to financial success and stability in life. According to his students, it was also a path of special interest for those who stayed with him.

In 1978, fourteen students enrolled in his AP Calculus course. Only five survived his rigorous expectations that first year, and only two of those achieved the necessary test scores to earn college credit at the end. However, by 1982, his course had 18 students, all of whom earned the qualifying test scores for college credit.

However, the Educational Testing Service®, who runs the test, questioned and invalidated 14 of the tests. Escalante, fearing that the inquiry came as a result of racism, then led a strong campaign to refute the ETS® decision. Ultimately, 12 of the 14 students re-took the test, and all of them earned a score of 3 or higher—all passing for college credit.

Perhaps the biggest take-away from Escalante's career is students don't need to be identified as "gifted" in order to have tremendous potential. As a new teacher of secondary students, I incorrectly believed that students would already be appropriately identified with gifts or learning disabilities when they came into my class. I didn't really comprehend that there was room for error in identification—and that, when an identification limited a student to fitting support, the results could mean disaster for that child's future.

Escalante realized that others in the school had unfairly underestimated the students he eventually helped to excel in math. When a teacher puts aside biases about race, socio-economic status, disability or behavior, they will discover many students who glow with sparks of understanding about complex problems. Helping those students to appreciate their own worth will in turn foster a love for deep and challenging learning—well beyond prescribed curricula—to develop their intellect.

We can start them on a journey of valuing themselves when we:

○ Know our students

○ Call them by their name

○ Listen to their stories

○ Show them that organic focus—even when the work is hard—pays off, and

○ Advocate for them when an injustice occurs.

According to his former students, these are the qualities that made Escalante such a great educator.

The second highlighted teacher of this chapter is LouAnne Johnson.

Most people know Louanne Johnson as the teacher portrayed by Michelle Pfeiffer in the 1990's blockbuster film, *Dangerous Minds* (Smith, 1995). While the movie was based on true events, Johnson would be the first to tell you that her original story played a skeletal outline for the film produced by Jerry Bruckheimer.

Although the movie is now considered one of the most egregious examples of "White Savior Syndrome" (where a white character portrays 'the truth and the light' to 'the poor, pitiful minority'), Johnson said, in a 2015 interview with *The Guardian*, that this was not the reality of her experience. In the first place, her classroom was far more diverse than the movie indicated—the Los Angeles neighborhood where she taught was not imbalanced with only LatinX gang members. Rather, she says, "In my class, the kids were evenly mixed: black, white, and Hispanic. In the movie they made it all minority kids with a token white kid here and there. That perpetuates this myth that only {and all} minority kids are at risk…" Nor, she says, did any students or parents call her out for being a "white bread bitch", as is portrayed in the movie. "Hell, nobody ever, ever said anything to me like that." (Clark, 2015).

Furthermore, anyone who has read any of Johnson's other books or follows her blog (she continued teaching for decades after the movie was made) will know that her educational goal has always been about teaching students to read, write, and think critically for themselves—never about swooping in to save them, as the white-savior syndrome suggests, but rather insisting they have access to challenging material and empowering them to control their own destiny. So, what is the takeaway from an educator like Johnson?

Because of the reputation of the movie, the truth of the takeaway is somewhat ironic: Johnson would tell us to look past our innate (and overt) biases that suggest a student can't learn challenging material because of his race or economic condition, their sexual preference, her criminal record or any other number of identifiers. In other words, do not let your bias influence your classroom decisions. I would hope that history allows those sentiments, and not the Hollywood movie that portrayed her as a 'white savior' to be her legacy.

Ultimately, Johnson believes that the core of teaching in any subject area must be Reading, Reading, and Reading, and she believes that students should be doing most of the talking and working in a classroom (Johnson, 2005).

If you want to know more about Johnson's work, you may want to read her teacher text *Out of the Box* and visit her website. She also has written a YA novel called *Muchacho*, which is used in many classrooms to spark conversation about diversity, identity, poetry, and growing up.

From my perspective, these two educators helped me realize some unintentional shortcomings in our identification and placement of the students in my classes. For example, when I was a very young teacher, I approached my classes with the attitude that those in advanced classes needed little support and those in my "mainstream" or remedial classes were not capable of high learning or exceptional achievement. It is a bias I am embarrassed to admit now, but it was one I needed to face in order to become a better educator.

Many educators and parents don't recognize gifted students unless they are high achievers in academic areas. However, as George Betts and Maureen Neihart articulated in their Profiles of Gifted, Talented,

Creative Learners, (Betts & Neihart, University of North Carolina, 2017) there are at least six profiles of gifted learner personalities, and unless we can begin to recognize all of them—not just those who present as "successful" because they are willing to play the game of school—we are unlikely to meet their needs.

The Six Personalities of Gifted; Betts & Neihart

I The Successful   II The Challenging   III The Underground

IV The Dropout   V The Double -Labeled   VI The Autonomous

(Based on the work of Betts and Neihart)

Students should also be empowered to recognize themselves as gifted. Sometimes, in our eagerness to properly place a student in an appropriate learning environment, we forget to include her in the conversation. In my experience, telling a student that she is gifted without helping her understand what that title means, or who she is, or how she learns can be counterproductive. Whether she accepts or rejects this adult-imposed label, she may not activate an internal exploration of her own metacognition because it feels out of her control. Over the years, it seems to have helped my own students to better understand themselves when they are exposed to the many possible manifestations of giftedness.

The figure below, which is based on the work of Betts and Neihart, indicates a list of identifiers and possible needs for each of the different types of gifted profiles. Utilizing research-based learning profiles from other resources, such as Myers-Briggs© or Emergenetics© can help students explore their own learning strengths and preferences.

Type I **The Successful**	**Type II** **The Challenging**	**Type III** **The Underground**	**Type IV** **The Dropout**	**Type V** **The Double-Labeled**	**Type VI** **The Autonomous**
Most often identified as GT	Many school systems fail to identify Type II gifted children	These students generally want to "hide" their giftedness.	Best described as angry with self, adults, and a system that has not worked for them for years.	Refers to gifted children who have a second identification flag such as second language learner, identified learning exceptionality, physical challenge, or emotional divergency	Have learned how to effectively manage the system (but not 'play the game') of school
Have "learned the system" of school	Divergently gifted.	Desperate to "belong" or "fit in"	Often feel rejected	Often do not exhibit behaviors that are traditionally associated with the gifted.	May also use the system to create new opportunities for themselves.
Have "observed" what works at home and school and behave accordingly	Typically possess a high degree of creativity	Deny talent in order to feel more included with a non-gifted peer group.	May present as depressed or withdrawn or defensive.	May have sloppy handwriting or disruptive behaviors	They do not work for the system; they make the system work for them.
Learn well and quickly and are able to score high on achievement tests	May appear to be obstinate, tactless, or sarcastic.	Sometimes appears as sudden and radical transformation from highly motivated and interested student	Frequently, have interests outside the realm of the regular school	Behaviors or disability may make it difficult to complete work	May frustrate their teachers with their seemingly "cavalier" or "I don't care" attitude.
Eager for approval, especially from those with power.	Often question authority and may challenge the teacher in front of the class.	Frequently feel insecure and anxious.	Fail to receive support and affirmation for their talent and interests	Often feel confused about their inability to perform school tasks	Have a strong, positive self-concept.
May be willing to get by with as little effort as possible.	Do not conform to the system	Dissatisfied reactions from parents or teachers increase their resistance and denial.	School seems irrelevant and perhaps hostile to them.	OR Frustrated with needs-based instruction rather than strength-based support	Have an intrinsic sense of success
Often miss discovering their own identity and desires; tend to "go through the motions" and seek both structure and direction from authority.	Have not learned to use the system to their advantage.	Respond best to be accepted for who and where they are at any given moment.	May have "dropped out" emotionally, mentally, and/or physically	Benefit from targeted remediation rather than blanket programming	Often receive positive attention and support for their accomplishments as well as for who they are.
Fail to learn autonomy.	Generally, receive little recognition and few rewards or honors.		May never be identified as gifted.	Can overcome many challenges with use of technology such as voice to text, text to voice/audio readings	Well respected by adults and peers
Generally liked by peers and included socially.	Interactions at school and at home often involve conflict.		Often appear bitter and resentful as a result of feeling rejected and neglected.	May show symptoms of stress or feel discouraged, frustrated, rejected, helpless, or isolated.	Frequently serve in some leadership capacity within their school or community.
May struggle with the inevitable changes that come with age and the world.	May feel frustrated because the school system has not affirmed their talents and abilities.		Usually very low self-esteem	May deny that they are having difficulty	Independent and self-directed.
Rarely actualize their potential because they rely on their success at "playing the game." rather than learning and creating.	Usually struggle with self-esteem.		Will benefit best from a working relationship with an adult they can trust.	May use their humor to demean others in order to bolster their own lagging self-esteem.	Healthy risk taker

Type I The Successful	Type II The Challenging	Type III The Underground	Type IV The Dropout	Type V The Double-Labeled	Type VI The Autonomous
	May or may not feel included in the social group.		Traditional programming is no longer appropriate for Type IV's.	Urgently want to avoid failures and are unhappy about not living up to their own expectations.	Strong sense of personal power.
	Some challenge their peers, and therefore are often not included or welcomed		Accommodations should be based on broad body of data driven findings	May be very skilled at intellectualization as a means of coping with their feelings of inadequacy	Do not wait for others to facilitate change for them.
	On the other hand, some have a sense of humor and creativity that is very appealing to peers.			May be impatient and critical and react stubbornly to criticism.	Able to express their feelings, goals, and needs freely and appropriately.
	Spontaneity may be disruptive in the classroom.			Benefit from strength-based programming	
	May be at risk for drop out or self-harm behaviors				

Adapted from Betts & Neihart

Beyond that personal understanding, gifted students should be supported with articulated, documented, specialized programming.

Gifted students have special needs in education for any and sometimes all the following reasons:

○ Gifted students, by definition, represent a very narrow population within a classroom, school, or community. In fact, their scores are typically in the 95th percentile of achievement or creativity or other cognitive abilities, compared to their peers. This makes them neurodivergent and unlikely to experience classroom instruction in the same manner as their classmates.

○ Also, in my experience, many gifted students disconnect from class when they already know the material or if they recognize that they could easily learn it on their own. As Del Siegel states in his "Gifted Students Bill of Rights" *Students have a right to learn new material every day* (Siegle, 2007), and the GT students I worked with craved this.

○ Furthermore, our gifted students will be best nurtured with autonomy and agency, rather than test-focused instruction. (Betts, Carey, & Kapushion, 2017). While the gifted students

I worked with enjoyed access to the challenging materials that "advanced" high school courses offered, they also needed support and nurturing in nearly all other aspects of their "being-ness". This "being-ness" includes executive function and emotional regulation—even imaginational regulation and focus and personal alignment with their own energy. In other words, advanced content is only half of the equation in addressing the needs of our gifted learners; while placing them in advanced classes or even college courses may be appropriate for some gifted students, for many it is simply not enough.

○ Yet another reason that we need to modify our instruction for gifted learners is because they are better able to learn in some ways than others. Below are my observations of different types of gifted students and their place in the diagram of Lev Vygotsky's "Zone of Proximal Development" (McLeod, 2020). Some of our more successful learners become extraordinarily anxious if they are asked to move outside of the center circle— what learners can do unaided.

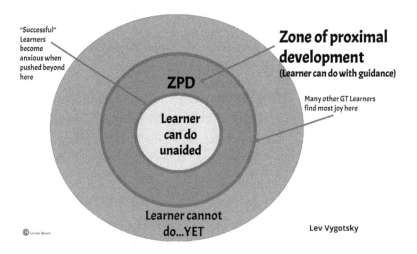

Looking back on the profiles of the Gifted Learner, we can see that many of our "successful" or "underground" gifted students aren't even *aware* that they are supposed to be learning something new in school (Betts & Neihart, 2017). Teachers sometimes don't recognize that they aren't challenging students because the students are so comfortable and successful doing 'what they know'.

On the other hand, I noticed that the "challenging" or "autonomous" or "dropout" learners preferred to live on the outer edge of the zone of proximal development. While these students need guidance for what is "inside" the zone of proximal development, they don't necessarily need or want that guidance from their classroom teacher. (Think of how people learn to master a video game—sometimes by trial and error, sometimes by asking friends, other times by reading the directions). These are the students who often become disengaged or disillusioned with direct instruction in school—or, conversely, when given the opportunity to chase their own creativity, they may develop scientific breakthroughs or artistic masterpieces.

Some students may even, by the nature of their "giftedness", be able to access something that falls in the far outer circle of Vygotsky's model—think about the movie *Rainman*© or a musical savant who can sit down to a piano for the first time and instinctively play something of beauty. Maybe they need to be getting educated in a completely different manner than traditional school offers.

It started with *Rainman*©. If you don't know the movie, it starred Dustin Hoffman and Tom Cruise, and it won four Academy Awards in 1989. In the movie, Charlie Babbitt (Cruise) discovers, after his father's death, that he has an adult brother named Raymond (Rainman). As it turns out, Raymond is an autistic savant—an incredibly brilliant mind trapped inside the need for rigid routine coupled with anxiety—who was living in a mental institution. Regardless of his ability to perform complex calculations in his head and retain a ridiculous amount of facts and trivia (he was a Jeopardy© whiz on his couch), Raymond was unfit to care for himself or survive the pressures of society. His obsessive-compulsive behaviors and his acute anxiety prohibited him from living outside the confines of a mental institution.

Raymond's story was an extreme case (and obviously full of Hollywood). Still, though I was only a year into teaching when the movie was released, he reminded me of a student I had worked with. We'll call her Aubree. She, too, had been institutionalized. I worked with her while teaching summer school at a lockdown detention facility for troubled girls. Many of the students in my class had been sentenced to years of incarceration for assault, armed robbery, even murder.

This girl was no exception—she was serving a sentence for aggravated assault as well. But she was different from the others. She was quiet and, though I didn't know it at first, she was *very* smart.

She was also non-verbal. In other words, she didn't speak. As I recall, she was about 14 or 15 that summer—they didn't group the girls by age or grade, just by "elementary" or "high school". She was in my high school class, but she was one of the younger girls. I had given a journal assignment at the beginning of the period, and I noticed that she wasn't writing. I asked her why, but she didn't answer.

"She don't talk," one of her classmates offered.

"Not ever?" I asked.

"I ain't never heard her," the girl returned.

"Well, do you write?" I asked—looking at her, but willing to take an answer from anyone.

"She don't have no pencil," her neighbor replied.

I gave Aubree a pencil and asked her to respond to the prompt. Instead, she stabbed the pencil through her hand so that it bled—badly. I had to call for a guard to take her to the infirmary.

A couple of days later she returned to class—with a bandage over the stitch in her hand.

Determined not to be intimidated by her violent act, I stopped her at the door and asked if she planned to participate. I told her she didn't have to talk, but I needed her to write.

"I don't care if you spell words correctly or if the sentences are complete. I just want you to write down your ideas like you hear them in your head. It doesn't matter what you write, but please write something."

Day 1 she wrote *"Something."*

So I wrote back: *"You stuck a pencil through your hand when you were angry. I think you have more to say than that."*

Day 2 she wrote *"I have a lot to say, but I don't think you can handle it."*

So I wrote back: "*Try me.*"

By day 10, this young lady was writing silver-tongued prose, describing a horrific childhood in a violent home. Her words painted powerful and genuinely painful images of physical and emotional abuse—so vividly that I felt abused after reading it.

Let me clarify—I did not teach this student how to write. She was already an excellent writer. Her ability seemed almost innate. Nor do I know if everything she wrote was true. It may have been. Maybe not. Good writers embellish, but fact can be freakier than fiction. It's hard to know and it didn't matter. Because we were in a lock-in facility, she was safe. As a rule, I had to report what she shared, but, as a rule, I received no follow-up reports of the validity of her stories or what action (if any) was taken.

What was impactful to me though, beyond the truth or fiction of her nightmarish tales, was the fact that she was such a good writer—by all measurements, a *gifted* writer. And she was in jail. And she had been willing to keep her words—her masterfully expressive words—to herself. I was a very new teacher—in fact, that day when she had stabbed herself was my first day in a classroom outside of student teaching. (*Welcome to your new career.*) This was a disconnect for me. At that time, in my world, gifted students were superlative students. They were excited about their brilliance and ready to share—even show off—to the rest of the world. This young lady wrote well beyond her years, but she was anything but a good student. After the first week of class, she diligently wrote in her journal every day, but she would never turn in a test or a quiz, she would never speak in class, she would never complete a worksheet on *anything*.

Her story was very different from the story of *Rainman*. His autism—not crimes or a violent childhood—kept him in a prison. Yet, their stories were the same, too. Both were incredibly brilliant, yet neither were fit to live among the free.

I couldn't help but wonder if anything could have changed that.

1988—the year I saw *Rainman*—marks the year that I began to speculate that many (if not most) gifted students are rarely our best-behaved students or our most achieved students. It was the year I recognized that, while some students don't do the work because they can't, there are many, very capable students, who just *won't*. Moreover, some of those students who "won't" are our best and brightest. Gifted students may, like Rainman, be suffering from a secondary exceptionality like autism or Asperger's or dyslexia, or, like Aubree, may be suffering from trauma or other emotional disorders. Years later, I would learn that these gifted students who experience inherent roadblocks to their learning are classified as "twice exceptional" learners. Along with second language learners, they may be the least likely students to be identified as gifted. As a result, these students tend to get left behind, failing to leave a blip on our radar as profound thinkers, and generally dropping out of school—either literally or figuratively. Some go on to achieve greatness without their education (think actor Robin Williams or Microsoft mogul Steve Jobs), but most do not. Some, like Aubree, spend a good amount of their life in jail; others may get a job that satisfies them and raise a family, while others live hand-to-mouth, paycheck to paycheck. It's hard to know.

This is the story of discovering the complexity of students. Of the stirring revelation that they don't simply come in four sizes: special ed, under-achieving, general, and honors. Of the questions I had upon learning that "Autistic Savant" was an actual condition—wondering how I would work with such a student if I came upon him in my future. Of realizing that my job was more important and complicated than I had ever dreamed.

I don't know what happened to Aubree. At the end of that summer, I moved to another state to start my career in earnest. Contact (outside of school) between teachers and students in detention centers was completely forbidden. Of course, I'll always wonder—did her life get better when she got out of the detention facility? Or did she grow into an adult like those in her stories? Did she understand the value of her gift? Did she have any idea how to use her words to open doors and change not only her life, but the lives of others? Or did she lack the skills to navigate into the realm of a professional?

It's impossible to know, but I guess I'd like to think she somehow became a famous writer one day, or even something less glamorous—maybe she went to college and got work in advertising or teaching.

I know the statistics aren't in her favor, but I stay hopeful. She's a middle-aged woman now. Maybe I've read one of her books or seen one of her commercials. Anything is possible.

What Aubree and *Rainman* helped me understand is that every student—no matter how quirky or difficult or angry or stubborn—every student has a story that is much deeper than his or her behavior. And every child deserves to learn both academic and affective skills to prosper in this challenging world.

While there may be requirements in place to identify and support gifted learners, there is no rule prohibiting a teacher from pursuing such goals with a student who has not been officially labeled as a gifted learner. In fact, the work a student produces for these goals could be placed in a portfolio which may then help them become identified or at least noticed and recognized by schools or other organizations as a high achiever.

The point is, just because a student hasn't been identified as gifted or talented doesn't mean that the possibility doesn't exist—if he asks for extension work, let him try it—the worst that can happen is that he fails to meet the goal...and failure is not failure. As Dr. Ken Robinson suggested in *The Element: How Finding Your Passion Changes Everything*, students must be allowed {even encouraged} to fail. "If we don't prepare them to be wrong, they'll never come up with anything original" (Robinson & Aronica, 2010).

Unfortunately, even *with* identified advanced learners, some teachers hesitate to allow students to take risks. Think back to the sentiments of Jaime Escalante and Louanne Johnson: We can't allow our innate biases to suggest a student can't learn challenging material...

This idea of saving students from failure was one of my most insidious challenges as a teacher. There were a fair number of days when I unintentionally held students back by telling them, "You can't do that."

Well, not those words exactly, but in an effort to keep a student from failing, sometimes teachers say things like this:

"You may find that book boring or too difficult—here's a book in your reading level."

Or

"Students who haven't mastered Algebra II skills aren't ready to look at calculus problems."

Or

"That's a pretty ambitious project—maybe you want to try something smaller."

This chapter is titled 'Discovering Hidden Gifts', and the take-aways are these: not all identified students are immediately recognizable as gifted, and not all students who are gifted are identified. So, if you truly want to help your students actualize their potential, get to know them, watch for their interests, learn their names and their stories, identify your own biases so you can look beyond them to see each student in a fair light.

And then, encourage them to pursue an interest that will engage them, and point them toward the tools to create, explore, find credible information, and record and reflect upon their findings.

CHAPTER 7

Agency and STEAM

STEM (Science, Technology, Engineering, and Math) has been an educational directive in the US for about 20 years. Unofficially, it started in 1957 when President Eisenhower launched the Space Race, but it was the 1990's before the National Science Education Standards were established.

Originally coined "SMET" (Science, Mathematics, Engineering, and Technology) the National Science Foundation (wisely) rearranged the acronym for studies in those fields to STEM in 2001.

Shortly thereafter, the "A" for "arts" found its way into the acronym. It may have been a desire to change the stereotypical belief that math and science people aren't creative, but more likely it was the value of collaboration, cooperation, and creativity stimulated by the arts that made this practice gain footing. Educators like Ruth Catchen, a STEAM Curriculum Development and Program Manager, as well as an artist-in-residence at the Jack Swigert Aerospace Academy in Colorado Springs, Colorado, feel that art integration to the STEM equation fosters creativity and encourages out of the box thinking for problem-based learning. "Having learning experiences that involve a variety of the senses will be memorable. It creates the opportunity to take those experiences and learn from them and apply them to something new. That is how innovation and creativity happen" (Catchen, 2013).

As a teacher of English Language Arts, theatre, journalism, and communications, I wasn't quick to join the STEM field. In fact, it wasn't until 2007 (some twenty years after I entered my first classroom), when a principal assigned me to assist our school's technology teacher on an overnight field trip (they needed a female chaperone), that I even began to understand the potential of such programming.

Technology Student Association® (also known as TSA) is an international organization dedicated to help students "learning to lead in a technical world" (Mission, 2021).

Every year, students from around the globe compete, first at their school level, then at the state level, and ultimately at the international level in hundreds of clearly articulated 'challenges'. That is, they are asked to critically analyze a specific problem and then conceive of a solution. In most cases, they are asked to then create that solution. In my humble opinion, it is a superlative use of problem-based learning.

In many ways, this was not a new idea to me. For many years, I had approached teaching from a student-centered perspective. I had learned from other clubs I had sponsored over the years that an inquiry and solution focused approach is a powerful strategy for teaching and learning. Student government or producing a school play or newspaper or yearbook could fairly be considered the original forms of both project and problem-based learning in education.

What makes this organization different though, is the sheer volume and variety of the challenges. Students can choose to study over one hundred STEM fields. There are the predictable areas like biology, environment, social sciences, construction, architecture, computers, manufacturing, and research; but there are also challenges in areas like debate, journalism, fashion, and leadership.

The other element of TSA that so intrigued me was the organized method of helping students manage their time and energy on their projects. TSA's model of the engineer's project notebook is the basis of the Project Notebook I eventually used in my own classroom, and which will be articulated later in this chapter.

After I began working with TSA, I endeavored to incorporate as much of their programming into my class as possible. Because they included rubrics with each challenge, and because the challenges touched so many areas of English Language Arts specifically, this was not terribly difficult. I offered up the challenges, but I also embedded the solution-seeking philosophy, particularly in the areas of curiosity and engagement and agency.

This practice was reinforced when I had the honor of listening to Dr. Jim Watters of Queensland University of Technology in Australia when he said, in his keynote speech to the World Conference for Gifted and Talented Children in 2017, that the secret to developing engagement in all students—but especially in gifted students—is to "combine autonomy with competence and connectedness" (Watters, 2017). This is as true for teachers as it is for students.

It is hard to understand why some schools or teachers seem to struggle with the idea of providing support for gifted students. Most schools are happy to develop and offer scaffolds and differentiation for any other type of student—unless they are gifted. When a gifted student needs help with organizing or planning or managing time or emotions, many adults tend to become frustrated and impatient; they may even question if the child is truly gifted! Often, students will report that the adults in their lives are annoyed with them and question their giftedness when they struggle with any of these things.

Perhaps the question going through many of these adults' minds is: "Do they really need help, or are they being lazy and/or manipulative?"

In my experience, most students need the help that they are asking for. Furthermore, when they don't need it, that is, when they are truly being lazy or manipulative, the game ends shortly after they get the attention they want. So, in either case, the best strategy for me has been to believe that they need support and just give it to them without judgement.

The reason I was drawn to this notebook is the flexible structure it provided my students. The intention of it is to give them a place to regularly return to that will ground them in their personal learning adventure.

It seems reasonable, when training adults for job-specific skills, that posting a learning objective is an appropriate strategy. However, when we do the same thing for students, it seems to me to take away the fun.

Telling the students what they will do before they do it eliminates the element of curiosity. This is not to suggest that teachers should teach without learning objectives in mind; of course we should! Nor does it imply that students don't benefit from some type of road map or agenda—many students do. But that information can be generally outlined rather than explicitly stated before beginning a study—and the notebook provides that outline.

Consider this: If I am baking cookies with my 8-year-old niece, I am not going to begin by telling her that 'today we will be learning to sift flour, double a recipe, and separate eggs.' Instead, I am going to invite her to make cookies with me! Together, we will read a recipe, practice hygiene, understand how to use multiple measuring devices, and self-assess by tasting the finished product. The engagement comes from the experience itself, and the learning is inherent. To solidify the learning, we will reflect afterward (over a glass of milk and some cookies) all the things she learned to do. Reflecting afterward in this manner is a far better strategy than previewing every skill to be learned in the lesson—ask any 8-year-old! Perhaps the next time we bake together, we can recall all the cool skills we learned the first time and which we will be applying for the next project.

Managing the balancing act of teaching is not easy work, and it is definitely not for the faint of heart. Sometimes, when I suggest that teachers allow a gifted student to pursue his or her own interest, or when I request that teachers offer extensions far beyond what the other students are doing, the educators ruffle at the thought of all the extra work. And who can blame them? They are overworked, underpaid and hardly respected, much less appreciated. If I could fix that with this book, believe me I would.

Since I probably cannot, the focus here instead is how to meet the needs of gifted students and still maintain sanity. Certainly, if a teacher had a strategy to efficiently and meaningfully support enrichment for their gifted student, they would do so. The notebook I describe here is not the end-all answer to meeting such needs, but it is a tool that my students and I have found to be helpful as they followed a personal learning extension.

The extensions I suggest for such students don't have to be the breaking point for teachers. When I began using this tool, I was teaching in a Gifted and Talented Center Program—an application-only option school-within-a-school, designed for students previously identified as gifted or talented. Since each of these students had an Advanced Learning Plan in place, they were all required to set and work toward one academic and one affective learning goal every year. That meant that each student in my classes created at least one project notebook a year. Some students would choose to do these independently and others preferred to work collaboratively.

Over time, I had classes outside of the gifted center and eventually worked with many gifted secondary students at numerous schools across my district. In those cases, the students completed their studies and the notebook in lieu of other assignments through one chosen course—determined by the school or the student. In other words, these deeper studies needn't be a requirement for every student in a general (non-center) class.

Most students in mainstream education are not going to have a need for such enrichment—remember, the gifted population is, by definition, only about 5-10% of your student total. The curriculum you have in place is likely appropriately challenging for most of your students. I would not recommend that this notebook be implemented and assigned to all students in such a class. Instead, pick a few pieces of the notebook that feel like a good fit for you and the gifted students you are working with—or better yet, allow the student who is working toward a learning goal to pick a few of the pages himself.

The Project Notebook

The Project Notebook is a tool that begins quite generically and can be modified as needed—it can even be modified by the student as s/he learns more about their study of preference. These next several pages are intended to help the reader understand how to use it most effectively.

With this tool, teachers who have students needing extensions could build an independent study into their curriculum and use this tool as a student research journal. The point of assigning it is not to give the student more work or the teacher a strategy for grading (although it can certainly work for the latter). Instead, and more importantly, the project notebook allows a student to pursue a passion as an academic, as a scientist, as an artist, as an entrepreneur—to document what they learn, what they need to learn, how they learned it, where they found it, and what they plan to do with their new knowledge. This journal and the accompanying artifacts that may go with it should be offered to the student *as a replacement* for much of the work (and instructional time) that covers what they already know. Rather than feeling like "more work," it should truly feel like an enrichment, allowing them to learn something new and engaging every day. And always, the focus must be upon the pursuit of curiosity and an expansion of understanding rather than an outcome or even the notebook itself.

Many students don't realize the hallmarks of what makes a person an expert in a field, nor what will be expected of them if they are going to do anything fulfilling or influential with their studies. They will find as they build something, market something, suggest policy, pursue employment in a field, discuss it—there is a common vernacular of those who work with it, there is a history of its evolution as a discipline. They may even want to consider how to explain it through multiple domains and across various contents. Ultimately, they will discover at least a rudimentary idea of specifically how a thing works (and what variations there may be), who are the experts, and/or what types of work the experts do. This notebook is the place where they can record their ideas and discoveries as they produce whatever it is that has them excited to learn. While they don't need to be mandated to do this beyond reasonable means for their age or ability, it's a great practice for any creator to begin early.

The Prompt

The notebook begins with an articulate statement of the assignment prompt aligned to the student goal. For greatest effectiveness, this prompt should include the project to be explored or the problem to be solved, the suggested types (or specific) resources to be used, the time frame for the project, and a suggested product or outcome of the work involved.

This is the same formula as the assignment slide included in the Unit Lesson Plan from Chapter 4.

This prompt may be developed by the teacher, the student, or (most effectively) a collaboration between both. Some examples of these prompts can be seen below:

The Prompt (Independent Sample)	I will be conducting an independent study about windmills. By the end of the study, I will have created a series of sketches or (my dream) I will have built a functioning 3D prototype of a windmill to be used at a person's home. This completed notebook will also be an indication of my learning.

The Prompt (Collaborative Sample)	Through improv, research, and original composition, our team will create and perform a script and 10–15-minute performance about the effects of culture, geography, and economics of a community. The script will include multiple styles of performance (i.e., reader's theatre, skit, monologue, slam poetry, etc.), original writing, work written by published authors, and some element of music. (This notebook is intended to demonstrate your thinking and learning processes.)

At its most basic, the prompt is a vision for the individual student or the team, articulating the expected work to be completed.

At its best, the prompt is a springboard for the learning adventure, as well as a point of clarity. It is a metaphor for focus—here is a place to come back to if our work begins to feel muddled or confused. Here is a starting point for talking if the student or team feels as though their ideas are ready for expansion.

The Table of Contents

The prompt is followed by a table of contents outlining the types of information the student might track. While this page begins as a directive list from the teacher, the student may also modify/personalize it for their specific final notebook. I have color-coded some sections of it for easier communication to the student. It is not at all necessary that every element on this list be required. As noted before, such a list helps students recognize the hallmarks of an expert in any given field.

Suggested Inclusions for Table of Contents

○ Sources (Final is MLA works cited but this is a running notes page)

○ Navigational Chart (Due Date)

○ Vocabulary and Associated Vocations

○ Formal Letter of Project intent (Due Date)

(NOTE: this letter can be used as a hard document of a student's ALP goal)

○ Supporting materials (at least 2 ● and 1 ✱)

• Organizational tools

(i.e., spreadsheet of roles and/or responsibilities, calendar, etc)

• Graphs, calculations, sketches, etc.

(Suggested images: patterns, trends, origins, parallels, convergences, contributions, etc.)

* Peer feedback and student reflection for revisions

* Copy of interview notes

* Surveys and data

* Flow Chart, Storyboard, and/or Script

○ Reflections and self-evaluation of process and product

Each of the suggested items in the Table of Contents are explained in detail in the next several pages:

Sources

The first item in the table of contents is the Sources. This is just a running notes page, using URLs or basic information for resources, but it can later be developed into an MLA Works Cited if that seems suitable. (One of my 6th grade students aptly called—and created—this page as a "Playlist"). Tracking sources as they are collected and used is valuable to a student as both a reporter as well as a consumer. In a functioning free society students should be encouraged as early as possible to credit their sources, and they should expect the same from the information they consume.

Many students (and adults) don't realize the importance and value of tracking their sources, which is why this tool is placed at the very beginning of our student journal.

Sometimes, because the Works Cited comes at the end of a research project, many students don't think of it until their project is finished… and by then, they've usually lost the valuable resources they accessed along the way. When it is the first thing they see, they understand that, from the very first article they read or interview they conduct, or video they watch, they must document every expert, every URL, so that they and others may go back to learn more and determine credibility.

In a world where information can be published and easily distributed to the masses with so little accountability, it is imperative to teach and review the pillars of credibility (accuracy, timeliness, point of view/bias, domain, authorship) frequently throughout the year—every year. As a language arts teacher, I directed students toward creating an MLA documented Works Cited at the end of their notebooks (it's easily created using a free app or as a function of a word processing program). While a formal Works Cited is best practice academically, each teacher can determine the priority for that element independently. For example, if your sixth graders are able to simply keep a running list of URLs, that may be enough to establish the credibility of their sources—they can learn to be more exact next year and the year after and so on.

Navigational Chart

This doesn't need to be a Know/Want to Know/Learned chart (KWL) as it was designed by Donna Ogle in 1986, but that would be a fine choice here. Regardless of how you or the student decides to set it up, the idea is the same. How can the student organize a visual chart of what she already knows about this area of study? What brought her to it? On what paths does she want to direct her energies to learn more? (Generally, students end up learning much more than they list here). Finally, every week or so, the student should take some time to reflect upon what progress she has made and what adjustments she may want to make as she moves forward.

Begin with a chart listing	K	W	L
What you KNOW (K)			
What you WILL KNOW (W)			
And			
What you have LEARNED (L) (completed after presentation)			
This is a running document, but it will be checked by teacher on (date or interval)			

In Elena Aguilar's book *Onward: Cultivating Emotional Resilience in Educators*, she laments that after her first year of teaching, she realized that she had an enormous list of things she didn't know in the field of education, and she celebrates that she also had an abundant list of new skills acquired. (Aguilar, 2018). Like the rest of us who are reflective, she discovered that such lists can be revised every single year—and for our students, encouraging such reflection every day or at least every week is likely a better interval for re-alignment. It is helpful for students to begin this reflective practice and also to begin in a place of confidence (this is what I *know already*; this is what I *have learned so far*) when they pursue deeper learning.

Vocabulary & Associated Vocations (or other lists)

The Depth and Complexity Framework© created by Sandra Kaplan and Bette Gould and distributed by J. Taylor Education, includes twelve icons, each addressing key concepts of study for researchers and academics. (Gould & Kaplan, 2020) In that context, this page might be referred to as "Language of the Discipline." As noted earlier, experts are well versed in the language of their discipline. It is important, for example, that a student who is discussing dance knows the difference between a plié and a pas de chat, or likewise, that a plumber knows the difference between an A Valve and a Vacuum Breaker. Collecting such terms provides the student with the ability to have a conversation (or write a manual) from the perspective of someone in the field.

The "lists" are not limited to vocabulary, though. They can reach into any aspect that inspires the student. Perhaps the student can instead create a list of jobs that a person with this interest might have, or a list of schools/programs for further study, or a list of historical 'influencers' or events from this field. This is a great place to be flexible and encourage the student to create a list that is most meaningful to herself.

Formal Letter of Project intent (and due date)

Because I taught middle school, and business letter writing was an expectation at this level, I often required a letter of intent with the project notebook. However, the assignment prompt can communicate a student's intent just as clearly. The value of the formal letter has two purposes though:

1. it offers students instruction in accessing templates and producing formal communication, and

2. it is a great place to record a specific annual goal, too.

I would encourage the formal letter to be used specifically to support students as they set their annual goals and consider how a particular project contributes to that. Many colleagues who don't teach language arts have found that a Google Form© does a great job of capturing these goals as well.

> Note: While some school districts have a strategy for documenting goals for student advanced learning plans, others are only in the developmental stages, with various levels of efficacy. Therefore, as a classroom teacher, you may find that you have either easy or limited access to these goals—or the goals may not even exist! When the access to students' goals is limited, I always recommend that teachers collect the goals for their own purposes. Then, if the district has a collection tool, I emphasize to students that duplicating this goal is not "cheating" but rather encouraged!

Before they write the letter, I generally ask students to focus their thinking about goals by helping them align with their personal vision of their future. Who is it they want to be in life, and what is something that interests them now? (I acknowledge that this vision will likely change for them in the future, but I encourage them to follow what attracts them *right now.*) In what manner would they like their teachers and counselors to support them? Whatever their long-term view, their goal is much shorter—no longer than this school year. (See Goals tables below for some suggested goals).

Academic/Career Goals	Product Suggestions
• Participate in a competition or event aligned with a personal strength or interest	• Multimedia or live presentation
• Submit 3 or more original works to contests for publication	• Portfolio
• Develop or use a practical application of one or more mathematical or scientific concepts learned throughout the year	• Website
• Complete work toward a career specific certification or a Seal of Biliteracy	• 3D model or prototype
• Work with a teacher to propose alternative products/ presentation styles for one or more assignments based on your strengths/interests	• Game
• Research, narrow, and/or apply for post-secondary opportunities	• Journal or Essay
• Create and/or launch a personal website, resume, portfolio, etc. to document your talents and achievements	• Self-Reflection
• Work with a teacher to incorporate one of your outside interests, strengths, or passions into a class project, topic, or unit	
• Document personal volunteer/community service work based on an interest or strength area	
• Become an active participant in an after-school club based on a passion, interest, or strength area.	
• Effectively complete advanced level coursework (high school credit for ms/college credit for hs)	

Social Emotional or Personal Efficacy Goals	Possible Steps Toward This Goal
• I will research and practice strategies for talking to new people • I will research and use strategies to improve my listening and/or communication • I will strengthen personal/peer relationships to effectively complete at least one collaborative project • I will conduct research and utilize tools to develop a system to manage my time effectively • I will conduct research and try new strategies to organize my materials • I will learn and practice strategies to cope with anxiety, depression, etc. • I will learn and practice strategies for self-advocacy • I will learn and practice strategies for perseverance • I will learn and practice strategies to be more flexible in thinking and/or responding to change	• I will find a trusted adult to support me with insight, resources, and feedback in this quest • I will conduct research using credible internet resources (videos, websites, etc.) • I will read books and articles about this subject • I will conduct research by interviewing individual people who have a strength or interest in this area • I will keep a journal or study notebook throughout my progress • I will find/create a method to practice daily personal reflection

If we are honest with ourselves and our students, we will acknowledge that very few individuals—adult or youth—find much success with annual goals. According to a study by clinical psychologist Joseph J. Luciani, Ph. D, only 8% of New Year's Resolutions are kept and 80% of them are abandoned by February. (Mills, 2020)

At the same time, we must also acknowledge that the pursuit of intrinsically driven creative endeavors—*personal goals*—are literally what gets a person through a day or a lifetime. Daniel Pink's book, *Drive,* details the positive impact that personal goal setting has on both motivation and progress. (Pink, 2009)

Whether it is for a day or a season or a decade, everything we begin has an end goal. When we plant a garden, we hope to see food or flowers as a result. When we know we want to build a birdhouse, we find the motivation to envision a design and bring together the necessary materials and begin construction. When we marry, we imagine the experiences we will have together as a couple.

Do things happen that make us modify or even abandon our goals? Certainly they do! It is the inconstant nature of life that makes it so important to nurture the belief in our students that they have some choice about determining their future so we can then help them develop the flexibility and resilience to adjust to inevitable change. They may choose to stay the path or change their direction completely, but first, they must know that they have a say—they have the power—to determine what it is they want in the first place.

To truly make this meaningful, we must encourage our students to take small steps toward something as big as annual learning goals, as well as be forgiving to them if they do not fully complete the goals. Again, emphasis should be upon the journey. I regularly ask students at the end of the year if they feel they made meaningful forward progress on this goal, rather than give any kind of mark based on meeting it or not.

Once the goal is set, the best way to nurture student agency is by having the student come back to the goal every week—have they made any progress? What might they do next? Do they want to revise or even completely change their goal? Why? What's next?

Some schools (including the one where I spent most of my career) base goal setting on George Doran's 1981 SMART goal model. SMART goals articulate learning or production targets that are **S**pecific, **M**easurable, **A**ttainable, **R**elevant, and **T**imely. Though Doran's protocol is likely very productive in the business sector, I discouraged its use with students. Specifically, when working with secondary students, the goals do not need to be *Attainable*. Consider this: how does a child know that something is unattainable? If we tell them, we are only enforcing the belief that "someone else" knows better. Why not allow them to investigate an idea for themselves and then adjust as they go?

I once had a group of students who set an academic goal of curing cancer.

They were 7th graders.

Rather than tell them "Maybe you should try something more realistic" they were allowed to gather all of the information they could about cancer. It only took a few weeks before they had learned that there are over 100 types of cancer and that it has been recognized (without a cure) since at least 3000 BCE. When they determined that a single school year might not be enough time to formulate a cure, they were allowed to re-evaluate. What about the goal intrigued them most? What would be an alternative? Ultimately, they ended up designing a video game to teach people about cancer, they organized and raised funds for the American Cancer Society, and they made a YouTube "draw my life" video about the causes and costs of cancer. The question we asked them at the end of the year is, "Did you make meaningful growth toward your goal?"

Their answer was a resounding yes. Though they weren't actually able to cure cancer at the age of 12, they learned many, many things. They learned about the types, causes, costs, existing and potential cures for cancers; they learned how to organize and promote a fundraiser; they learned how to make a stop action video called "Draw My Life, Cancer Edition" (Collins, 2014), and post it on a social media platform; they learned how to work together and how to endure disappointments and celebrate successes together. As a result, these students found new interests and lifelong pursuits including a study of medicine, film, art, and community service—not because they were told they had to, but because those things naturally arose from their own agency—their own voice in determining one step forward followed by another and another.

The letter of intent gives the students both a starting point and a point for final reflection. It is their mission and vision for this short project, giving them a place to go back to when they are lost or need new direction as well as a barometer to help them measure their personal growth once the project is finished. But it is not the measurement for success.

Supporting Materials

Here I ask students to supplement their journals with various new tools that we've learned how to create throughout the year. To keep it manageable for the student, I encourage them to only select 2 items from List A and 1 item from List B. The idea of this is to apply the material we are learning to their area of interest, which, ideally, increases their engagement in mini lessons and instructional standards.

Because they are expected to include them in the notebook, this list can be modified as appropriate, and students can receive direct instruction for different skills as necessary.

List A	List B
Organizational tools • (If working in teams, spreadsheet of roles and/or responsibilities and deadlines, pillars of work, etc.; if working independently, a calendar breakdown of personal and imposed deadlines) ***Graphs, calculations, sketches, etc.** • (Suggested images: statistical representations, patterns, trends, origins, parallels, convergences, contributions, blueprints, designs, fabric patterns, etc.)	• Peer feedback and student reflection for revisions • Copy of interview notes • Surveys and data • Flow Map, Storyboard and/or Script (if there is a presentation portion to their work)

Reflections

○ Personal reflection around collaboration

As mentioned before, some classes have enough students looking to fulfill advanced learning goals that it is both sensible and beneficial to have them work collaboratively. When that is the case, students may be well served to have each team member reflect on their own contribution, the contributions of others, and the effectiveness of the whole team. This is a place to post that reflection. This could be a single reflection at the end of the project, or a collection of reflections done throughout the process.

○ Self-evaluation of process and product

Whether the study is collaborative or independent, scholars, artists, and entrepreneurs should often be encouraged to take time for reflection and personal evaluation of their work. As in the group reflection, support should be provided to guide the student so they can focus on their strengths and their successes.

This is also a good time to allow the student some agency about how the reflection is presented. Is it a short essay? Is it a drawing or a thinking map? Is it a poem or a graph? Is it a meme? As with the prompt itself, this is a great place to suggest one or two possible formats to the student, and to follow with "or any other way that feels right to you."

One of the unexpected benefits of this tool came to light during the Covid 19 Quarantine of 2020. Teachers who understood this tool were able to assign meaningful work so their students could conduct some self-study at home. As a result, these students, who reported differing levels of engagement with *school,* reported continuous engagement with *learning.*

It turns out that the most important jobs we have as educators may be to give students the navigational tools necessary to gather and disperse credible information and then help them find the direction they wish to go. We don't always know their destination, because in many cases, it hasn't been discovered yet. What I've determined after all these years of working with students is this: If education is working correctly, the end goal is still unknown to us because it will be a new iteration and an evolution of what has come before.

CHAPTER 8

Playing to Learn
(Game Theory and Hanan al Hroub)

Hanan al Hroub is a teacher who has recently been celebrated because she recognized that students must be supported to have a readiness to learn before learning can begin. She is the 2016 recipient of the Global Teacher Prize, which was the result of her instructional philosophy described in her book, *We Play, We Learn* (Hroub, Teaching for Peace in Palenstine, 2016). The methods she uses in her classroom are designed to address academic instruction for students who have experienced trauma. Her solution for trauma-aware instruction is to incorporate as much play into class as possible. She also proposes that, while competition can be healthy, when it is employed with students who have experienced trauma, the opponent should never be the classmates, only the clock or the teacher.

Palestinian-born, Hanan al Hroub was raised in a refugee camp in Bethlehem, Palestine. A victim of trauma herself, Hanan decided to become a teacher to help children overcome trauma after her own children were witnesses to a violent shooting that injured their father. Afterward, the girls, who were ten at the time of the incident, became withdrawn, sometimes aggressive, and unable to participate in learning at school, so Hanan kept them home for a while.

Determined that they would continue their studies, Hanan created a corner in the room of their small apartment and began making card games and other toys to help the girls play and learn at the same time. She realized then, that when the girls were in this safe space and preoccupied with playing, they were learning without even knowing it. They were also becoming less aggressive and more cooperative.

That is when Hanan decided to become a teacher. She designed her classroom to be full of games that had learning at the center. Often, she noticed, her students were learning not just math facts and reading skills, but also skills for collaboration. Because the challenge was either "students vs the teacher" or "students vs the clock" rather than "students vs students" she helped foster the value of working together. It was not unusual for a student, once he had completed his own task, to then help his classmates conquer their tasks as well.

The idea of "play" is broad. As a verb, it means to "engage in activity for enjoyment and recreation rather than a serious or practical purpose." (Play, 2021) It can also mean taking part in a skilled activity, such as "I play softball" or "I play the violin." Synonyms include "enjoy", "relax", and "engage". Wouldn't life be wonderful if everyone at school was enjoying, relaxed, and engaged every day? How can we work to make that sort of environment in our own classrooms?

Like al Hroub, I also loved to incorporate games into my classroom. Over the years, I discovered that the most efficacious games were those that didn't always have "right" answers. Instead, the games posed problems that had myriad possible answers (students were celebrated for "out of the box" thinking) and also "pretend" games. So, while my students often enjoyed games like Jeopardy® or Headbands® or Twenty-Thousand Dollar Pyramid® or Kahoot®, we also employed a lot of theatre improvisation and dice games, such as:

Sell your Book Commercial:(The Intro Game)
What's Needed: A common text for at least a small team of students have read

Object: Use the skills of Hook, Summary, and/or Thesis to create a commercial that "sells" your text to the class.

This can be done as a quick skit at the front of the room, or it can go bigger and become a slideshow or video.

- ○ Start early in the year by having students summarize a text they had read using the old rules of twitter—140 characters or less.

- ○ As hook strategies are acquired, students can create improvs for this alone, or combine them with summaries

- ○ The same is done for thesis statements.

Jigsaw Tableaus (Multi-Intelligence Shakespeare)
Object: Create short summaries of text as physical and visual "still shots"

○ Read a scene of a play or a single chapter of a book

○ Establish 3 key moments that mark the essence of the text

○ Play them out as "still shots"

  • Use a student narrator to give a short explanation of each tableau

Journalist on the Street
Object: Explore character traits

Materials needed: Costume or prop box

○ Each student is assigned/chooses character from text

○ Students collect 2-3 items that "match" their character from prop box

○ A designated "interviewer" asks questions generated from the text

○ Students answer in character

Target Number:
This game requires:

○ four regular six-sided dice and

○ one 12-sided die.

Object of the game: Use 4 dice to create an equation that equals the "target number"

The *rules of play:

○ Roll all of the 6-sided dice
   Put these to the side

○ Roll the 12-sided die
   This is the Target Number

○ Use any and all math applications you know to create an equation with the 6-sided dice to equal the Target Number

○ Share/Compare answers

In a remote setting, this can be done with padlets® or another cool app

OR

students could write their answers and hold them up to the camera

Rules can be modified based on student ability

As an example, let's suppose we rolled the first four dice and came up with

○ 6, 3, 3, 2

Target Number: 6

In that case, here are some possible solutions:

$$\frac{6+(3+3)}{2} \qquad (6 \times 2) - (3+3) \qquad \{(6 \times 2) - 3\} - 3$$

As you can see, students will recognize with this game that there are multiple ways to approach and express pretty much any problem and solution. In my experience, students find this to be kind of a fun game and a teacher I know brings it out when there is a little down time at the end of a lesson, or it can be used for students to find partners—team up with someone who made the same statement. Sometimes, during a long transition, he'll have a student come up to be the "dice master" and the rest of the class will play. Usually, 'props' is given to the student or team that finds an answer that is different from the rest of the class, although everyone with a correct equation is celebrated.

What's interesting about this and other dice games, is that it seems like it's all left to chance—and much of it is—but the players are also allowed a lot of personal agency. That is, they get quite a lot of control over how they interact with the dice they are given. And they can see that there are numerous methods to answer a simple math question.

Another cool thing about a dice game like this is that the more you learn and know (about math in this case) the more agency you get. You can see that if I only understand addition, subtraction, multiplication, and division, I have limited ways to arrange these numbers. I may not even come up with an answer!

But if I understand exponents or factorials, I have a wider range of possible answers.

$(6/2 \times 3) - 3$ $\qquad$ $2(3^2 - 6)$ $\qquad$ $3! - 6 + 2 \times 3$

This is a wonderful way to illustrate the concept that growing one's ability also increases their personal agency.

This game is a GREAT common experience to refer to when discussing the idea of agency with your students because, as in video games, we don't all have to take the same path to get to our school designated finish line—nor will success in life look the same for all of us (in fact it will be unique for each of us!)

Hanan al Hroub determined that creating a classroom full of games would invoke the happy inner child from her students. (Hroub, 2016). The intention of games such as those above is to relieve the stress of "school" and correlate the idea of learning with a sense of enjoyment, relaxation, and natural engagement. It demonstrates that practicing or exploring anything—whether it is a specific skill, a set of facts, or some much bigger concept can be joyful. So many people believe that only small children want to engage in play, but the truth is that role playing and improvisation is entertaining for all people, young and old. More importantly, it not only requires but also develops critical thinking, communication, and social skills. Best of all, what has seemed to be true in my classes is that when people are laughing and having fun, they are more likely to remember information generated at that time.

The take-away from Al Hroub? She tells us to keep agency alive as a meaningful conversation in your class by engaging in as much play as possible. Enjoy the games listed here, and give yourself permission to play, too; enjoy your own creativity in this arena. Find, invent, and celebrate play in your room whenever possible by digging back to the TV game shows of your childhood or the board games you played at your grandma's or ask the kids what's hot in tech and party games and modify them for your classroom.

The best form of playing generates a perpetual revisitation to the idea that learning is individual and, rather than looking for exactly the 'right' answer all the time, each of us should instead pursue our creative problem-solving self. Students of all ages can put away the pressure of achievement and connect to their true inner desire to simply expand thought when they play.

CHAPTER 9

Fourteen Strategies to Support Gifted Learners

Dendrites and learning

Those of us who have been in the business of education for more than 25 years have witnessed something that is simultaneously terrifying and exhilarating. That is the rapid evolution of instructional styles and their outcomes. As recently as twenty years ago, only about 10% of high school students advanced as far as Calculus AB, but as instructional practices have improved, so have the number of students who take advanced maths—current trends indicate that 16% of high school students will finish calculus by the end of 2021. What is more impressive is that we also have students advancing as far as Calculus III, IV, and even some who are taking (and passing!) Linear Algebra before graduating high school.

The reason we find this exhilarating is obvious: good instruction has led to students finding greater academic success. Cue the applause button, because that kind of success flies in the face of negative press about schools.

On the other hand, although the result is great news for students, the evolving nature of instruction can be overwhelming and frightening for teachers—especially seasoned teachers who have perfected a process to run efficient classrooms.

But change is natural and inevitable, and in order for students in all schools and districts to truly have access to accelerated material and skills, the most enduring teachers and schools must regularly modify and extend their instruction to meet the needs of all their students—including the most highly gifted.

Brain research conducted as early as 1979 (Buell & Coleman, 1979), has shown that brain cells with more dendritic branches create more possibilities for synaptic connections—which causes a brain to learn more efficiently. How might our secondary schools mirror such branches within programming—allowing for more creative connections for their gifted learners? It may be easier than you think. This chapter will offer 14 programming techniques to take back to your schools as early as tomorrow, providing support, complexity, depth, and novelty for the gifted learners in your community.

Let's start this exploration with an understanding of very basic neurology. An elementary concept for how the brain works is that it is composed of neurons, which are specialized cells transmitting nerve impulses—or nerve cells. Within these cells are dendrites, a word borrowed from the Greeks, meaning "trees", because dendrites literally look like miniature trees. Each neuron has many of these short, branching fibers that extend from the cell body. These fibers increase the surface area available for receiving incoming information. So, dendrites with many branches indicate a brain that is receiving and storing a lot of information.

Much like trees, what we know about dendrites is that the branches do not just "appear". They are fed from a root system, up through the neuron into the dendrite stem, and that is what causes the branches to grow. It would follow, then, that gifted students would have larger dendrites—that is, dendrites with many more branches—than other students, which in turn create more possibilities for synaptic connections.

In true transparency, I don't know if this is how gifted brains truly work (I am not a brain scientist!) however, I appreciate the image as it relates to learning institutions. That is, it seems to me that schools that most effectively support highly gifted learners would allow myriad possibilities for all kinds of learners. How can our secondary schools develop and mirror such extensive branches within programming— allowing for more creative connections for their gifted learners?

Hold that image—of the neuron providing energy up the trunk of a dendrite and then branching out from it—to understand the proposals in this text. For none of the instructional and programming ideas that will be suggested can be expected to simply "occur". In order for learning to be effective and for a system to change in a classroom or a whole school, my experience has shown me that change must follow a dendritic path. *It must build on what was there before.*

Much of this chapter was created with the collaboration of one of my former students and, later, colleague, Ben Hershelman. As resource teachers, our job required us to oversee the entire gifted population of each of our assigned schools—we have rosters of identified advanced learners that can easily exceed 1200 students (and often reach much higher) at the secondary level annually. It is impossible for us to directly affect each of those students or support and monitor the progress of their learning goals. It is likewise a challenge for any individual teacher in a secondary school to be the sole provider for the advanced learners there. But systems and practices can be implemented easily if we follow the metaphoric "dendritic path" of an individual school's current programming. We created this list of suggestions to help school administrators and teachers implement gradual and palatable changes that might provide exponential support for gifted learners who otherwise may not have their needs met.

Mascot Time

One very simple example of this is the elevation of what we call "Mascot time". Most of our middle and high schools have some type of advisory period (usually named after their school mascot) scheduled for some or all students. While there are many bits of business to be done through this class period, not to mention student study time, this is a natural place to start with whole school Advanced Learning Plan (ALP) support. Generally, when we ask schools how these classes are populated, their answer is that the computer randomly generates the rosters. What we have proposed (and what has begun to work in a number of schools) is that several of these sections of advisory are designated as ALP-specific. In other words, all students who currently have an ALP are funneled into sections led by teachers who have volunteered to take on some of the GT support duties.

In these ALP specific advisories, students learn about the purpose and value of goal setting. They also investigate their own 'locus of control' and think about goals they can work toward intentionally. Then, the goals are collected in this class. Students also do a quick weekly check in to report on the progress toward their goals, and they close out their goal report at the end of the year. Two other collateral benefits of the ALP-specific advisory are that students are given time to discuss ideas with like-minded peers, which is considered a best practice for GT instruction. Additionally, this is a great platform for sharing GT-specific announcements (around contest, scholarship, and travel opportunities) with this special population. Some schools also use this time to present social/emotional lessons that are specific to the needs of gifted students, or they have the students pose questions for a relaxed version of Socratic Seminar. (It doesn't have to be relaxed, but it seems to involve more students when it is free of grading and a required number of contributions.)

This is just one of more than a dozen suggestions that we will pose. This particular strategy may not work for your school, especially if there is not currently an advisory period in place. However, many schools are currently re-thinking how they can build such a support system in their school, and it would be wise to keep in mind the needs for all students and group them accordingly if such a plan is implemented. As Covid-19 encroached, several of our schools found that creating an ALP specific online course through Schoology© or Google

Classroom© was a good system for disseminating announcements, collecting goals, and sharing lessons for a school's total identified gifted population.

Interest-Based, Goal Focused Learning

As has been stated throughout this text, another strategy to embed across all curricula is the idea of strength or interest based, goal-focused learning. This is accomplished at the most basic level when students craft these for their personal advanced learning plan at the beginning of each year. We suggest encouraging secondary students to set this goal with a *personal interest* in mind, rather than simply their learning strength. When they do so, they tend to pursue the goal using their strengths naturally. Although the collection, monitoring, and completion of student-selected goals is still a work in progress, we hear more and more from students that this process feels more meaningful to them, and they have greater interest in learning to self-advocate as well as learn new skills and ideas through this interest-based pursuit.

Literature Circles

While lit circles are an everyday skill for elementary teachers, we have been surprised to learn how few secondary teachers feel comfortable with this strategy. That is a shame because this is an excellent tool for helping students develop a sense of autonomy and to become engaged. While teachers who do employ literature circles in their classes are surprised to hear that many don't, some of the arguments I hear from reluctant teachers include, "I don't know all of the books they will read" or "How do I know if they are telling the truth?" "They won't learn the vocabulary I want them to learn," and "It's just too much work."

I can appreciate these concerns. Honestly, before I started using lit circles in my classes, I had the same apprehensions. When I was a very young teacher, the lit circles I had seen modeled included a list of study questions generated by the teacher (well, they weren't really generated by the teacher—they were usually designed by a book publisher and printed up by the teacher.) Obviously, coming up with a list of study questions (and their answers) for an unknown variable of book titles would be a formidable undertaking. This is less daunting if we change our approach to text discussion. Perhaps we shouldn't be in the business of having students read simply to correctly answer a set of questions created by an outside entity.

One of the most valuable things about lit circles is that the students can read texts of their choosing and learn to generate questions of their own at the same time. This is a great opportunity to discuss depth of knowledge, levels of questions, and Bloom's taxonomy with your classes. It's also a great time for them to start thinking beyond the surface—of course we want them to understand details about characters and setting and plot…but how is this literature an expression of the human experience? How does it relate to science or history or culture? Or how would it be expressed in mathematical terms? It is not necessary for every single unit in an ELA class to revolve around lit circles, but it would be a good practice to include at least one unit where the students have choice about the texts that they are reading each year. If a teacher is still reluctant, it would be a good idea to collect data around student engagement for a unit. Several of the teachers who I have worked with have done so (using pre and post surveys and test scores as measurement) and have been pleasantly surprised with the data showing increased engagement from their most dis-interested students.

Social/Emotional Bibliotherapy and Brain Trusts

One of the greatest benefits of the lit circle is the opportunity students have to hold intellectual conversation with each other, without the constraints of classroom-imposed structures (you must contribute x number of times, etc.). In a similar fashion, students can have such intellectual discussions around social emotional units or 'brain trusts'. In our department, the secondary counseling team has developed numerous multimedia text banks that revolve around particular social emotional themes or topics, with the intention that they could be utilized through advisory classes. The original intent was to address social and emotional issues through literature story lines—for example, we might utilize the Emotional Wheel (Karimova, 2021), Gestalt Theories (Perls, Hefferline, & Goodman, 2013), Amy Morin's *13 Things Mentally Strong People Don't Do* (Morin, 2014), or any number of texts and tools around social emotional learning to analyze the characters in a story rather than only using literary devices or structures.

Gestalt Theories (adapted from (Perls, Hefferline, & Goodman, 2013)

Similarity	Items with shared characteristics are perceived as being connected
Continuity	Items aligned with one another are perceived as being visually associated with one another
Closure	The brain tends to perceive forms and figures in their complete appearance despite the absence of one or more parts
Proximity	Items placed close together are perceived to be part of a singular item
Connectedness	Elements connected by uniform visual properties are perceived as being more related than elements that are not connected.

What Ben and I have discovered is that these short lessons can be applied to many classes, and they are a good source for opening meaningful, relevant conversations in lots of content areas. Why not present the social emotional lesson about suicide prevention in a biology class when studying the biological effects of depression on the brain and body? Why not have a conversation about what it means to be gifted within the context of understanding community and the evolution of societal structures and roles throughout history?

 Most ideas taught in school can (and should) cross through many lenses. Why not do so with social emotional lessons as well? The same can be said for literature. Wouldn't it be something if every course included a lit circle unit that related to the topic(s) being studied in that content? For example, I enjoyed Ken Follett's *A Place Called Freedom* very much, but it would have been even more engaging if I had read it while studying about the discontent of the British working class in 1768 as well as colonial history. Likewise, students who are studying (or experiencing) obsessive compulsive disorder or Asperger's syndrome in a psychology class might find an enriching connection to books like *Turtles all the Way Down* by John Green, or *The Curious Incident of the Dog in the Night* by Mark Haddon.

When we recommend and allow discussion time for such books as they connect to our curriculum, we are offering much needed support to our gifted students. We are creating dendritic branches for our classrooms and our students alike.

Student Openers

We borrowed from a few GT Center teachers when we introduced the idea of student openers. Other teachers I know have used similar strategies and called it '5 Minute Professor' or "My Random Knowledge Moment'. This is a viable opportunity to extend what a student knows to the things s/he can learn about any subject, but in the spirit of community building, they don't need to connect to anything but the presenter.

The basic gist is that every class period opens with a short student presentation that brings a little bit about themselves into the classroom. Using Depth and Complexity© or Content Imperatives©, students develop one or two key follow-up questions to make connections from their own lives to the course content. Three days a week, students are assigned to give a 10-minute presentation on something of interest to them. Usually, each student presents two or three openers per semester.

Topics have varied from video game strategies to interesting stories about a grandparent, to student business ventures, to tree frogs or butterflies.

The incredible thing about an opener is that it gently brings students who are otherwise disengaged into the community of the classroom. This is an activity that allows students to bring a piece of themselves—something they may not even have to research—to the class. They can use any number of presentation methods; some students create slide shows while others make videos or Prezi's© or Kahoot© games, and others just present something live (even in remote conditions) like introducing their dog and the tricks he can perform. It's very low-investment, low risk, and it creates a strong line to help students connect to learning, school, and each other. One teacher I worked with intentionally included some errors in his examples at the beginning of the year to foster conversation about how the creator could avoid such blunders *and* how the audience could address those blunders appropriately.

And while it seems to the student that she isn't doing anything academic, she is, in fact, working on numerous skills that foster intellect—they are organizing a presentation and getting in front of an audience; they may be engaging in digital technology, often learning skills in that arena as they go. For many students the only thing that feels academic is that they are asked to pose a question to their classmates at the end of the presentation using the content imperatives from Depth and Complexity©.

One of my favorite "opener" stories is about a student who is a selective mute; that is, he has chosen to be non-verbal as a result of trauma he experienced when he was very young. I had followed this student for several years, and he had rarely spoken in that time. Even when he did speak, it was never louder than a whisper. In his first semester, he refused to even participate in openers, but as time went on, his teachers nudged him to at least write his response to the questions others posed. Then, he started thinking about putting an opener of his own together. His first presentation was a slideshow with captions— no speaking at all. By his sophomore year, he started to open up to a few of us who worked with him and used what I call his big voice. At that time, he made a presentation about his hobbies. Next came video games that he liked to play, and from that grew a small club of students who met weekly to play the games. The openers literally allowed him to take the necessary baby steps to become engaged in class and eventually become part of the community.

Flexible Scheduling

Sometimes our schools are providing exactly the right structures for gifted students, and they just don't realize it. One example of this is flexible scheduling. Virtually all the schools in my district allowed for online learning, well before the remote conditions of during Covid were imposed, but they rarely advertised this as an accommodation for their gifted students. As early as sixth grade, students in our district can take an advanced course via our district's Virtual Academy (or local community colleges) while sitting in another teacher's class—and they have special scheduling and even offer limited transportation to get high school students over to our career and technical education centers during the school day. In the years before the quarantines, some of our schools had already gotten even more creative, building in "flipped" instruction, when students and teachers were allowed to work from home on a designated day each month, or "Flexible Fridays" when students must report to classes only by special request from their teacher. This type of scheduling was designed to free up other students to conduct field work on their goal-centered studies or contribute to a community service project. Schools who already had such asynchronous structures in place had a much easier time of addressing the special needs of remote learning that began in March of 2020.

We also suggested counseling students out of classes that they are simply taking as "place holders" and encouraging them to find meaningful content in their everyday courses. If that means connecting to a local community college to take more complex math or science coursework when they are high school juniors, then schools should accommodate them to do so. Certainly, this won't be suitable for all students, but now that we have seen the massive reach of online instruction, this may be something attainable for many more schools and students.

Clubs, Contests, and Activities

Another opportunity that schools offer to their gifted students (but is often overlooked as an asset) is the variety of clubs and activities offered after school. Many of our gifted students report that their involvement in speech and debate, or technology student association, or theatre, band, yearbook, athletics, etc., is the most enriching part of their day and the reason that they come to school or engage with the work of school. It is important that schools, families, and students recognize the value of such sources as they plan for their personal learning goals. Regardless that these activities do not have a testing valuation, the soft skills being learned in such programs cannot be over-emphasized: clubs and activities are a critical aspect of our children's education, and they generally offer the kind of agency and autonomy that a gifted student needs to survive.

Other school activities and local or national contests, especially when their work is offered in lieu of something that a student has already mastered, can provide experiences far beyond what our school curricula conceives.

Here are some great examples of students who were encouraged to follow a path to discover their personal purpose—a trail to 'Arete' if you will.

- ○ Olivia Hallisey, who won the Google Science Fair at the age of 17, with her creation of a rapid test for Ebola (Raymond, 2016).
- ○ Wolf Cukier, who, as a 17-year-old intern at NASA, discovered a new planet 3 days into his work there (Esfandiari, 2020).
- ○ Lucress Mourima is a student in Lehigh Valley, Pennsylvania. She, along with other black students who make up about 5% of their school's population, have started a Black Student Association at their school and have also insisted on sharing a different (and more complete) perspective than their school's social studies curriculum was teaching about slavery and modern-day structural racism (Dwyer & Merlin, 2020).
- ○ Boyan Slat, a 19-year-old who has developed a system to clean plastics out of the ocean (Dawson, 2020).

These students didn't develop such agency because someone asked them to consider their ultimate purpose on earth, but rather, they arrived at these *moments* of Arete because someone invited them to explore their personality and recognize their strengths, and then encouraged the confidence in them to follow their interests for *this* step forward and *this* step forward and *this* step forward.

We encourage schools to utilize these programs and to celebrate them as part of your gifted programming when talking to students and parents.

Mentors

As mentioned earlier, meeting the needs of a heavy roster of gifted students can be overwhelming for teachers, and often a school simply doesn't have enough support staff to assist an advanced learner with meeting an academic learning extension—especially if it is lofty or technical. (One of my schools once had a student design a machine that could levitate material using sound waves—way out of our league!). This is where mentors can help. A mentor provides knowledge of a particular field, wisdom and experience, perspective, affirmation, and inspiration to students who have discovered an area of passion. Because it is of extreme importance that schools bring in only safe, vetted, and appropriate mentors to work with their students, we sought out (and were able to find) some organizations that already offer such services. Specifically in Colorado, we suggested looking into <u>CoMentor.org</u> as well as local <u>Retired Teachers</u>. Other states have similar organizations that are worth looking into.

Another way to connect students to valuable mentors would be to partner with a local college to help students there earn practicum hours while also providing a source of strength to a small group of gifted students, possibly directing a play, helping with a class project, a mini study unit, or some other community activity. It turns out that many university undergraduates and postgraduates are delighted to work with students by taking a small group on a Saturday geology adventure, leading a group to help with kitchen work at a food bank, directing a play, judging technology contests, or conducting a small group literature study unit.

The Final Four (Universal Strategies)

The last four strategies in our list are practices we would hope all teachers would do in all classes for all students—and especially for our gifted students.

Post-Secondary Prep & Digital Portfolios

Although meeting the needs of a high number of gifted students can be challenging, there are simple tweaks to all content areas that could result in a big payoff for gifted students. One such practice is to enhance the emphasis on post-secondary study programs.

Post-secondary study and preparation seems to be placed in many high school ELA curricula, but often not until the senior year of high school. This is far too late for students to truly take advantage of many opportunities available to them. Furthermore, much energy has been diverted from college entrance exam prep in some schools (especially in lower-income schools, we've noticed). This puts all students at a significant disadvantage. While gearing instruction toward SAT questions would be inappropriate, all students should develop a strong skill set to recognize and acquire vocabulary and know the basic math skills that the SAT tests—not because they are on the test, but because they indicate literacy.

 Students who show aptitude in early grades (9,10) should be encouraged and afforded opportunities to study test taking strategies and even practice for the National Merit PSAT in the 10th grade. The 11th grade PSAT awards National Merit Scholars with financial support and many colleges will offer additional funding based on a student's National Merit status. Even students who plan to follow a vocational career path after high school should be primed for community college admission, as that is where most required technical certifications must now be earned. If students were spending some time in each of their classes to create portions of their digital portfolios or conduct research on post-secondary opportunities, more students in general would be prepared for life after high school, and many would discover that they want (and *can*) pursue meaningful study beyond high school.

Reflection

Perhaps even more important than post-secondary research being offered in every class, is that every class offers intentional student reflection at the end of each period, or at least at the end of each week in each course. This needn't be a formal, written journal, but rather a system of reflection that is meaningful to each student. It could be written for some, drawn in doodles for others, expressed mathematically, in a spreadsheet, or digitally recorded. According to Hattie's Table of Effect Sizes (Hattie, 2018), student self-reported grades registers at 1.66, which is pretty darn impressive if you consider that anything over .4 is a significant positive contribution to learning. While there isn't a definitive effect size for "Student Reflection" per se, we know from such accomplished gurus as Lev Vygotsky (McLeod, 2020) and also Robert Marzano (Marzano, 2019), that reflective thinking is a key component to student learning. Furthermore, a study from Worcester University concluded that reflection "allows {students} to develop a realistic sense of efficacy and motivation. In addition, it will develop their metacognition so they will be able to set and monitor the achievement of realistic goals." (Colley, Bilics, & Lerch, 2012)

Consider the implications of allowing students time to regularly reflect on their learning in all classes! This is a relatively simple practice that could have exponential rewards.

Backward Planning

Another "across the school" strategy that every teacher could employ as a support for gifted students (and all students, really) is helping them understand how to backward plan toward due dates.

While some teachers will post a due date for assignments and leave it at that, we have found that most teachers offer support for getting to deadlines by planning the whole thing out and then sharing the dates with students. What would be more effective is to teach the life-skill of backward planning for projects, in the same manner described for teacher planning in Understanding by Design (Wiggins & McTighe, 1998). In other words, instead of simply assigning students check points and due dates, help them brainstorm the steps they will need to complete before the deadline date and then give them time to figure out reasonable deadlines for themselves. This fosters the life-long skill of personal planning.

Teachers generally employ three steps for backward design of study units, and we have found that students generally need at least four:

1. Identify and record the problem, due dates, and presentation requirements.

2. Establish academic structures for saving and sharing research.

3. Follow the problem-solving model, and

4. Create the presentation of findings.

Explicitly teaching these steps and holding students accountable to the deadlines they create individually or as a team is an excellent way of truly supporting the executive function skills that so many of our gifted students lack.

Building Relationships

The last universal strategy that we encourage is also the very first rule that we believe all teachers must establish for a healthy, effective classroom: Building Relationships.

In our observations, most effective and virtually all good teachers know intuitively how to build healthy and supportive relationships with their students. In our roles, we are fortunate to find many, many teachers who have very special bonds with their charges. We will list several strategies that these masters employ, but it is important to recognize that, at the root of all these strategies is the educator's desire to sincerely value and connect with each of their students and to be a font of strength and inspiration in their lives. Teachers who approach their work from this threshold generally tend to be excellent teachers and almost always find tremendous joy and fulfillment in their work. Here are some of the strategies they employ:

1. They have special names for every student. Beyond that, they remember every student's name—in most cases, for many, many years after they have graduated.

2. They have the students create and post some personal statement about themselves. It may be a personal coat of arms or a resume or a motivational, guiding quote. This helps them understand their students' strengths, goals, and interests.

3. They play. Whether it is before or after class or part of the classroom instruction, these teachers know that people who play together tend to stay together, so they employ games and imagination—even if it is just rock, paper, scissors—in their everyday interactions.

4. They check in with their students—when they ask, "how are you today" (and they ask every day), they are truly interested in the answer.

5. They send notes—whether on a postcard or at the end of an essay they grade, these teachers make a special point to *reach out* (not just give feedback) to their students with the written word.

6. They listen.

7. They allow their students to make mistakes with dignity—they understand that just because a student is gifted doesn't mean he is perfect or must be good at everything.

8. They don't expect their students to prove that they are gifted.

9. They don't take it personally when a student knows something the teacher doesn't know.

10. They model the behaviors and attitudes they hope their students will one day have.

11. They set clear boundaries and respectfully maintain them.

12. They look for the good—what are the students getting *right*— and they celebrate that as a strategy for further learning and improvement.

13. They say good things about their students to others—parents, co-workers, and other students (though never as a comparison).

14. They are honest and frank, but never mean-spirited.

15. They allow themselves to be vulnerable with their students.

It is also important that students develop a connection to the school. That can't happen if they don't find connection with the teachers and each other, but it can be enhanced with rites of passage for every grade level, as well as intentional transitions from school to school and grade to grade. Virtually all schools do this to some extent, but the schools that are best supporting their advanced learners are including those students in the planning and presentation of these ceremonies and protocols. Furthermore, they include explicit instruction to help students learn how to interact with each other and how to encourage their peer community to interact with them in return.

As we reflect on the image of the brain's neurons stretching out in dendritic branches, creating a dense forest of energy and ideas, we can imagine the powerful value of such growth. While there are many implications that brain development will eventually lead us to in the field of education, we have chosen to only consider it from a figurative example in this chapter. Specifically, you are asked to think about how you can capitalize on the programming options you currently have in place, and then imagine how you can build extensions from those systems to better support your advanced learners. Ultimately, if a school hopes to support its gifted learners and give them opportunities to truly flourish, the practices and systems to help them succeed must be stretched in all directions through the school. It is not enough to only encourage autonomy or connectedness in one classroom, nor should a teacher believe that merely offering advanced curricula (without social, emotional, or personal management skills) is enough to meet the needs of the gifted. By extending the opportunities and strategies described here throughout the entire school, all teachers will be increasing the surface area available for supporting gifted learners.

Chapter 10
Practicing Teacher Agency

Although the idea may feel a bit new and foreign and requires a certain level of "letting go", most teachers can embrace the idea of nurturing student agency because they see the value it adds to the lives of their students and to the greater idea of a true, healthy democracy. A community, nation, or world that is designed with *people* in mind requires a populous that has a sense of personal importance, choice, and consequence.

Nurturing agency for oneself, though, often proves to be a bit more challenging.

If we return to the idea that student agency means:

○ The student has control over significant choices in his studies

○ Those choices have consequences in the real world and

○ The student has enough information to anticipate and/or explore those choices and consequences.

Then it would follow that teacher agency is this:

○ The teacher has control over significant choices in his classroom

○ Those choices have consequences in the real world

○ The teacher has enough information to anticipate and/or explore those choices and consequences.

However, in my experience, many teachers don't feel that they have control over the significant choices in their classroom. Many would argue, in fact, that the very example of Socrates that I used in chapter three proves that exercising his personal agency as a teacher not only had him jailed but ultimately executed! And that would be an understandable argument.

But it wouldn't be an accurate argument.

Because even though Socrates was sentenced to death for encouraging his students to think, he continued down his chosen path. And while death may seem like an unreasonable choice or an undesirable outcome for self-empowerment, it was nevertheless a personal choice on his part. He could have at any time, renounced his position, reversed his practices or even quit his job, but according to Plato's *Phaedo*, Socrates chose instead for his grave sentence to be his final lesson to his students. (Plato, 2012)

Most teachers I know who are experiencing any kind of angst in their career feel as though they have lost one or more of those elements of personal agency.

While this chapter has the potential to develop into an exploration of the age-old theme so often contemplated in high school and college, which focuses on determination vs free will in our own lives, I'll try to offer more than that here. It was a question that we mostly had stopped worrying about by the time we were in our thirties, I suspect, because we had careers and children and homes to manage, and such deep contemplation was either out of reach or out of style.

The idea has been masticated since the beginning of human literature in any case. I always enjoyed having students read Oedipus Rex or Antigone specifically because these stories raise the question so well—Are we masters of our destiny or slaves to our predetermined story?

Of course, we needn't reach back so far to find literature that raises such a question—hundreds of authors from Shakespeare to Stephen King have explored this theme.

Michael S. Gazzaniga argues in his book, *Who's in Charge*, "neither neuroscience nor philosophy have yet to decisively determine whether free will exists" (Gazzaniga, 2011), which is pretty much how any discussion I've ever facilitated or been a participant in regarding this debate ends. Most likely, each of us can look to our own experiences and indicate events that were established as a result of our personal choices (even in the face of seemingly random events), while other situations appear to be predetermined. Nothing we did or could have done would have changed the outcome. The truth likely lays somewhere in the middle.

As we try to establish our own personal agency as teachers then, we must consider and foster the things we can control, and then focus our energy on the sense of empowerment that comes with voice and choice.

One of the challenges that I encountered as a teacher was the constant pendulum swings in educational pedagogy—at the national and state levels, and even at the school level—new principals often seemed to bring in their own agendas. While I love the dynamic nature of change, I also found it difficult to adapt to numerous instructional requirements in a short window of time.

For example, I find tremendous value in assuring that students can read and write and perform complex computations and uncover mysteries using the scientific method. I also think it is imperative that we have effective, qualified teachers in every classroom. As a result, I find it important to use student data and teacher observations to ensure that schools are efficacious. However, in the last twelve years that I taught in my own classroom, I had five different principals, each basing their teacher evaluations on different benchmarks, and just as many different standardized tests that my instruction was supposed to align to. Even for a teacher like myself, who rarely reused a lesson without significant revision, this was disorienting and unsettling.

Once personal life issues of marriage and caring for children and parents and navigating health issues and political climate was added to the mix, the work became overwhelming and un-sustainable. There were many, many days when I, as well as most of my colleagues, felt to be on the breaking point. In circumstances such as these, teachers feel constantly threatened by burnout.

In my 34 years of teaching, I have encountered some very good teachers who managed to endure these challenges and others who ran from the profession. In *Onward: Cultivating Emotional Resiliency in Educators*, Elena Aguilar has included a very extensive list of the traits and dispositions of resilient teachers that I encourage any teacher to read. (Aguilar, 2018)

In my own, simplified experience, teachers who survive such difficult times seem to align themselves with a sense of purpose, creativity, and ever-forward expansion. Additionally, they ground themselves in the following:

1. Meditate daily (formally or informally)
2. Remember your purpose
3. Reach for the next best idea and feeling
4. Give grace

Daily Meditation

People who know me know that I have long practiced time for contemplation in my day. Whether it is meditation or prayer, a session of mindful exercise, a time for creating music or some other form of art, teachers must set aside time for themselves to slow down and recharge their battery every day. Maybe it comes from eating lunch alone or writing in a journal first thing in the morning or taking a long walk after school. No matter how you do it, establishing time to contemplate what you do and why you do it is critical for surviving the demanding career of an educator. Furthermore, this must be a conscious effort every day because it is nearly an impossible ask. Just as we must schedule time into our day for grading papers and reading emails, we must schedule time into our day for daily self-care.

Fortunately, even if you don't feel comfortable joining a church or other community support group, we live in a time when access to meditation instruction is easier than it has ever been. There is a plethora of free guidance videos on YouTube©, apps are readily available on your personal device, and almost all fitness trackers have complimentary guided meditations with upgrades available.

I have found that even a three- or four-minute session of deep breathing or stretching can get me both re-focused and energized enough to face any class or parent meeting or presentation with ease and confidence.

Looking back on my life, it is easy to pinpoint the times when I didn't offer myself this daily space, and, without fail, these were challenging times that adversely affected myself, my family, and my students. Conversely, even when I was experiencing the stress of caring for a dying parent, finding time to meditate daily allowed me to stay grounded and focused. Just as people are instructed on airplanes to put on their own oxygen mask before assisting others, teachers also need to take care to ground themselves and find personal balance before they can manage the difficult work of guiding gifted children toward their potential.

Work with your intention in mind

Hopefully, you did not choose to become an educator because it would be an easy job. (If you did, you've made a terrible error in judgement and now is the time to look for a new career!)

In all likelihood, you became a teacher because you love working with young people and watching them pursue their potential.

When you approach every day with the intention that you have chosen this career to enjoy the supportive relationships you are building with your students and facilitating an environment where they can chase their own imagination, creativity, and capability then you will stop feeling the stress of your work and instead feel joy.

Some days are more difficult than others, no doubt. One of the many endearing qualities of teenagers is their unpredictability and ever-changing direction. There will be days they don't like you or even appreciate you. There will be days when they let you down, but there will also be days that they make you proud and joyful beyond words. Teachers who learn not to take personally the whims of their students—while still being respectful of their students' needs, feelings, and ideas—will find the most fulfillment in this role.

One rather silly, but effective, strategy I used as a teacher was to keep a small vase in my room with a little water and one or two flowers. (I'd have kept a whole bouquet, but fewer flowers kept the price down.) At the end of the day, I would empty the water out of the flower vase, and as I poured the water down the sink, I imagined that it had absorbed all the negative words and actions that may have occurred in my class on that day. As a result, I rarely felt as though I had to take on any of that negativity. It reminded me that my intention was to have a classroom where people could chase new ideas and explore healthy relationships. When I washed the negative parts of the day down the drain, I recapped one or two good things that had happened as well. Staying grounded in what is working gives a solid foundation for moving forward.

Likewise, one's love for the career must not be conditional on the political or administrative environment in which they are teaching. Teachers who place the burden of test scores or evaluation expectations ahead of the individual needs of each student as a person are bound to find themselves feeling powerless and downtrodden. We simply cannot raise scores when students are not in a place of learning readiness. Furthermore, they cannot maintain learning readiness year after year if their understanding of personal agency is not nurtured.

This is not to suggest that all tests will or even should go away. While it is likely that testing will evolve over time to measure growth and ability in a less formal and less invasive manner, one cannot question the necessity for using scientific methods to determine if teachers are effective and students are learning necessary life skills. In the same vein, one cannot argue that "life skills" will remain constant over time either. The lesson in this is to take the tests results as a single point of data in the big picture of your work and your worth. As recently as ten years ago, I would develop anxiety hives as a result of the stress I absorbed around state testing. I would have been far better off if I hadn't given my power to such measurements. Testing periods and test scores were not the final word in my career portfolio.

Similarly, if you have already dedicated yourself to learning the craft of your instructional area, you are likely an expert and you have much guidance to offer your students in the form of mini-lessons and coaching. Know that. Own that. Your job is to focus on feeling the best about what is happening in your classroom. Let your own feelings be the barometer of your classroom's success.

When we approach our daily work with our purpose in mind—the determination to provide fertile ground where students tap into their inner resources and creative inspirations—we can let go of our concern for arbitrary and fleeting numbers. And generally, student growth and skill acquisition fall into place.

But in order to preserve a consistent sense of personal agency, we must stop worrying about the myriad measurements of our value that are imposed by higher forces. Just as we tell our students to pursue their learning for the sake of the experience, the knowledge, the growth that comes with it—and to stop focusing on the grade—we must embrace those same things about our work in schools.

Our gifted students, identified and unidentified, do not need us teach them to behave best, nor do we best serve them by filling their minds with all the things that we know. Gifted students are best served by creating and failing and creating and failing—and creating yet again. When we design classrooms which allow for that, we are devising an environment that best serves a society that is integrated, intelligent, and thriving. This is work that will never be done. It is important, perhaps above all, to learn to enjoy each moment of the experience that is happening in your classroom. Teachers have a daily opportunity to reach for our own arete and maintain an oasis of leading-edge creativity and inspired interaction.

Reach for the Next "best thing"

Sometimes—often—you will be asked as an educator to teach or use something outside of your expertise or comfort zone. Perhaps it is content you have not had to teach before or maybe it is a technology platform that you've never used before. If you are like most teachers, you have found that your school's grading program is constantly changing, and it is difficult to keep up. For many teachers who were teaching in the 1990's and early 2000's, the move from creating poster board projects and dioramas to utilizing digital platforms was intimidating and cumbersome. When schools had to move to online instruction literally overnight in the face of the Covid 19 quarantine of 2020, teachers everywhere were scrambling to figure out how to work in virtual classrooms and deliver meaningful instruction to their students in an entirely new way. Those who survived and thrived during these seemingly insurmountable trammels did so because they embraced the opportunity to explore their own creative problem solving—and those who rigidly adhered to previous (or newly imposed) specifications about instructional delivery found themselves flying off the wheel.

Whether it is an instructional quandary or an emotional low, it is important for you, as an individual, to reach for the next "Best Thing".

The teachers I know who have best survived the torrents of a career in education are well versed in both old and new pedagogy and they are also in touch with their emotions. In other words, they model the behaviors they would like to see their students adopt. At their best, they are emotionally grounded, life-long learners.

Of course, no teacher is at her best every day, but great teachers aspire daily (or at least weekly) to put aside time for perusing professional texts and journal articles, reading literature that inspires or entertains them, or exploring new technology. That is, they fill their bucket and hone their craft. They engage in ongoing professional development both formally and independently.

Also, great teachers find their best work comes from careful and diligent preparation. Flowers and vegetables do not flourish in gardens that have not been nourished correctly, and neither does student creativity. The very best facilitators have a clear roadmap of every school year, every semester, every unit, every week, every class period—and while they allow for flexibility and adaptation along the way, the energy and coherence of their course is based in the stability of this vision. When something isn't working the way they hoped, they modify their instruction or their structure or their class time, or whatever their observations and gut suggest is the next best attempt at meeting their students' needs.

Daniel Siegel's book *Mindsight* explores the value of functioning as an optimally integrated system in our daily interactions. He suggests that those who will endure under perpetually changing situations must be flexible, adaptive, coherent, energized, and stable. (Siegel, 2012). When we practice these habits, they not only increase our own sense of agency, but they also model a healthy approach to life for our students.

An equally important competence that teachers must cultivate is a connection to their own emotional state. I can say unequivocally that the times when I struggled the most in my career were not when I was unhappy with a particular administration or schedule or curriculum, but rather when I neglected to *notice* that I was unhappy. When teachers pay attention to their emotional state, they have a better opportunity to navigate change for their classroom and their life in general.

Just as we help students understand core emotions, we must recognize our own state of emotions and design actions to pull ourselves up when we find ourselves in psychological discomfort. Everyone works best when they recognize a challenge and are focusing on solutions.

My personal image is that of a "lifeline" trailing into murky water under a boat.

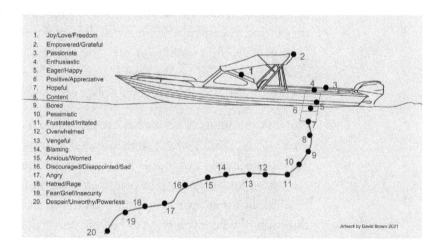

The deeper water represents my most oppressive emotions—all of which I have felt at some point about my work in education. The point of the image (which my husband drew for me to post on my office wall) is not to tell me to jump from the bottom of the rope to the captain's seat in the boat, but rather to remind me to find a better feeling than the one I am currently experiencing. Although the ascent from the depths needn't follow one knot after another (it's okay to skip a few at a time), it is much easier to pull oneself away from an awful feeling by simply reaching for something that feels just a little less bad.

For example, anger is not an emotion I want to sit in, but it feels better than sitting in grief or despair. And once I can get to a place where I'm feeling angry, it is not a difficult step to blame someone for my troubles. Of course, blaming someone or planning for revenge isn't very healthy, but I can pull myself to a better spot by acknowledging that I'm just frustrated or pessimistic. When I spend too much time in my own pessimism, it becomes rather predictable and boring. But when I'm bored, I can usually find something that I'm content with, and that usually makes me feel appreciative, and so on. With this blueprint, it rarely takes long to pull myself out of the water and into the boat, and eventually in the captain's seat, where I find that I am joyful and feeling a sense of freedom.

I realize this is an unorthodox and perhaps even naive approach to changing one's mood, but the point is that it works for me and allows me to be more effective as a teacher and more productive. Some may suggest that I should embrace my bad feelings, but for me, I don't find that sitting in despair serves me well. It may not be a tactic that works for everyone, but it works for me. The teachers I know who are successfully practicing agency have a system in place that pulls them out of emotional turbulence and into a place of empowerment and control.

Notably, this image takes me back to Daniel Pink's ideas from his book *Drive* (Pink, 2009), which were introduced in the preface of this text: Set your goal and reach for it—not in one leap—but step by step. Figure out where you are going. The place you move yourself to next may not be ideal, but is at least better than where you were before, and in the direction of where you want to be. Success of all kinds tends to come in small increments, and that may be the most important concept we can embrace as teachers and help our student to learn.

Grace

In its most human sense, grace is defined as "mercy" or "pardon"; kindness and courtesy; a sense of courteous goodwill. Without a sense of courteous goodwill toward our students, we cannot expect to earn the same from them, their parents, or our administrators.

While Dabrowski's theory of positive disintegration (Tillier, 2009) suggests that growth cannot occur without tension and challenge, it does not dictate that those oppositions must come from the classroom teacher. In fact, such circumstances come so naturally into the world of a teenager that it would be superfluous for a teacher to feel that he needs to add to the heap. Additionally, when our students make errors in judgment or struggle to understand what they need to do, we must recognize that they need help, not a scolding. Whenever possible, teachers should see themselves as a source of stability and strength for their students—a beacon of gentle direction during a storm.

Similarly, if we cannot offer grace to ourselves, we will never achieve a sense of agency—of having control over the challenges that present themselves to us. There will be difficult students and parents, there will be difficult administrators and political climates. If trends continue as they have for the last 4000 years, it is unlikely that you will see tremendous riches from your public-school paycheck. There is little that compares though, in knowing that you had a hand—sometimes an incredibly significant hand—in supporting a future entrepreneur, astronaut, physicist, or just generally good person. Being angry with ourselves and the communities we work in stifles our ability to manifest good things in our lives or the lives of others. As my mother would say, if you want to make change, do good and show your best.

In its divine sense, "grace" suggests an unmerited assistance for regeneration. Sometimes the "next best thing" means a move to a new place. Although moving to a new school or even a new career can be hard work, it may pay off in ways we cannot imagine. When a teacher finds herself in a place of oppression and limitation, she has two choices—pull herself out of the feeling or move away from the environment. If you are spending time in daily self-care and focusing on your intention and purpose, the right move will show itself

In my thirty-year career as a classroom teacher, I made several moves early on. One move, seven years into my career, brought with it a $10,000 reduction to my already skimpy salary. In the long run, though, it allowed me to raise my children closer to my extended family as well as to work in and ultimately retire from an excellent school district.

One of my colleagues once quipped that he had spent much of his career—if not his life—getting "kicked to the next best place." He had left a school where he had taught with me for about five years because he was very unhappy with the administration. A few years later, he confided that he had not wanted to leave that school community, but he felt that he had exhausted his ability to work with the newest administration there. In the long run, he had landed at a school where he was given some new assignments that revitalized his creative side more than anything had in his previous role.

Final Words

Just as one would do in a video game, the exploration of the consequences of our choices will not always result in smooth sailing to the finish line. But we never come back to a game without the knowledge we acquired on the last turn. This is as true when we foster agency for ourselves as well as for our students.

Teaching with agency in mind will be a theoretical shift for some educators, and tools alone will not be enough to empower students fully. To truly nurture student agency, we, as educators, must believe that our students are capable and wonderful human beings who are in the process of growing toward their fullest potential. We cannot give up on them (or allow them to give up on themselves) when they make a mistake. We cannot allow them to embrace their errors or negative behaviors or struggles to paint their self-portrait. In order to provide students with agency, we must assume a growth mind-set and help them build such a mindset as well.

We must also examine the possibilities of building on what has come before. Some seasoned teachers may read this book and ponder "isn't this all the same old stuff?"

And yes, this book is examining pedagogy that began millennia ago. But hopefully, chapter by chapter, you have been able to see an evolution of those ideas over time. Ideally, we are constantly stretching forward with instructional strategies, and hopefully we are ready to do so much more quickly than education, as a system, has done in the past.

This anecdote reaches back to the earliest part of my career.

We had just finished an in-service on Cooperative learning. One teacher, Dovey, who had been teaching for about 20 years, was kvetching that she had just wasted another hour on a recycled topic.

Another teacher, Martha, who had been teaching for over 30 years, said, "You just can't use that word, recycled. Or repackaged. Think of it as an additional perspective, or better yet, an evolution. We can't say that Cooperative Learning is new, but it's not all old either. Look for one thing to try (that's different).

Martha's timely and sage advice was recently articulated in Brene Brown's book *Dare to Lead*. She basically says, 'you know that it's exhausting to be the smartest person in the room. So, stop assuming that you are!' (Brown, 2019). Brown's advice to listen to change is important to our own stability and to the expansion of our work. What is a significant modification to an idea from your professional team or even your students to what you already know? Or what is a need that can be fulfilled as you move forward?

In fairness, the cooperative learning session that Dovey was frustrated by, or agency, as we've been discussing in this text, are not new ideas. As we've seen, teachers—great teachers—have been employing strategies to support agency since Socrates used them in 490 BCE!

If you are a new teacher, hopefully you will find a strong foundation for your new career in these pages. If you have a good amount of experience behind you, it is my wish that you consider a new technique or methodology you can add to your craft. If Socrates were here today, hopefully he would find something very new to try, too. When we move toward the future of education with student agency in mind, we can imagine, create, and implement so many new techniques! Think of the possibilities:

○ Remote learning has opened the opportunity for students to have more agency in the courses they select. While only one school in an area may be able to offer German or Calculus, students no longer need to be limited by transportation barriers.

○ Also, students can have a greater voice in the educational path they choose to follow. While many students can continue to acquire all the prerequisites for traditional post-secondary schooling, schools and districts that focus on student agency can also provide connections to more immediate job skill instruction, such as professional certifications and licensing offered through community colleges.

○ When we consider the cumbersome nature of standardized tests through the lens of student agency, we can imagine that one day (soon!) growth can be digitally embedded and measured through mass data collection of nonintrusive activities—the way that fitness trackers or Khan Academy© do now.

Carl Sagan famously said in his book, *Cosmos*: "You go talk to kinder-gartners or first-grade kids, you find a class full of science enthusiasts. They ask deep questions. They ask, 'What is a dream, why do we have toes, why is the moon round, what is the birthday of the world, why is grass green?'

These are profound, important questions. They just bubble right out of them.

You go talk to 12th graders and there's none of that. They've become incurious. Something terrible has happened between kindergarten and 12th grade." (Sagan & Wageningen, 1981).

When we work with student agency and the pursuit of curiosity in mind, we will foster both independence and motivation in our students. Using a history of excellent teaching strategies as a foundation, we can utilize and create new tools to hone our craft even more. We can modify our instruction to reveal to students that they do have control over significant elements of their learning, and those choices are meaningful. And until they can collect enough information to recognize the consequences of their choices, we can illuminate and celebrate each students' individual value to themselves, their community, and the world in a way that is neither overwhelming nor suffocating but rather empowering and motivational.

Fostering the gift of agency will help kindle the flame of enthusiasm and wonder for them, so they may find and actualize their own potential.

References

"State Model Evaluation System". (2019, September 4). From CDE—Colorado Department of Education: https://www.cde.state.co.us/educatoreffectiveness/statemodelevaluationsystem

"What is Giftedness?". (2021, July 12). From Davidson Instititute: https://www.davidsongifted.org/gifted-blog/what-is-giftedness/

40-40-40. (n.d.). From TeachThought: https://www.teachthought.com/wp-content/uploads/2016/03/404040.jpg

Aguilar, E. (2018). *Onward: Cultivating Emotional Resilience in Educators.* San Francisco: Jossey-Bass.

Betts, G. T., & Kercher, J. K. (1999). *Autonomous Learner Model.* Alps.

Betts, G. T., & Neihart, M. (2017). *University of North Carolina.* From Profiles of Gifted, Talented, Creative Learners: https://uncw.edu/ed/aig/documents/2017/profiles%20of%20the%20gifted%20talented%20and%20creative.pdf

Betts, G. T., Carey, R. J., & Kapushion, B. M. (2016). *The Autonomous Learner Resource Book.*

Blanchard, K. H., & Broadwell, R. (2018). *Servant Leadership in Action: How You Can Achieve Great Relationships and Results.* Berrett-Koehler Publishers.

Brown, B. (2019). *Dare to Lead Brave Work: Tough Conversations, Whole Hearts.* Edbury Digital.

Buell, S. J., & Coleman, P. D. (1979). *"Dendritic growth in the aged human brain and failure of growth in senile dementia." Science (New York, N.Y.) vol. 206,4420 (1979): 854-6.* From National Library of Medicine/PubMed: doi:10.1126/science.493989

Catchen, R. (2013, March). *"Reflections - How STEM becomes STEAM," The STEAM Journal: Vol. 1: Iss. 1, Article 22.* From The STEAM Journal Vol. 1: Iss 1, Article 22: DOI: 10.5642/steam.201301.22

Christine J Briggs, e. a. (2008). A National View of Promising Programs and Practices for Culturally, Linguistically, an dThnically Diverse Gifted and Talented Students. *Gifted Child Quarterly*, 131-145.

Clark, A. (2015, August 14). *"Dangerous Minds at 20: has the Ultimate White Saviour Story Aged Well?"".* From Guardian News and Media: www.theguardian.com/film/2015/aug/14/dangerous-minds-at-20-has-the-ultimate-white-saviour-story-aged-well.

Colangelo, N. (2002). *Counseling Gifted.* From National Reseach Center for Gifted and Talented: https://nrcgt.uconn.edu/newsletters/fall022/

Colley, B. M., Bilics, A. R., & Lerch, C. M. (2012, January 2). *"Reflection: A Key Component to Thinking Critically.".* From Canadian Journal for the Scholarship of Teaching and Learning : https://doi.org/10.5206/cjsotl-rcacea.2012.1.2

Collins, A. (2014, January 14). *Draw My Life, Cancer Edition.* From YouTube: https://youtu.be/g4gVsnyG3rE

(2014). *Colorado State Model Evaluation System for Principals: 2012-2013 Pilot Report.* Colorado Department of Education.

Colvin, R. L., & Edwards, V. (2018). *Teaching for Global Competence In a Rapidly Changing World.* Paris: Organisation for Economic Cooperation and Development.

Dawson, C. (2020, October 9). *"A Dutch Inventor is Cleaning the World's Most Polluted Rivers in and Effort to Save the Oceans.".* From CNN, Cable News Network: www.cnn.com/2020/10/09/world/cfc-boyan-slat/index.html

Dawson, P., & Guare, R. (2009). *Smart But Scattered: the revolutionary "executive skills' approach to helping kids reach their potential.* Guilford Press.

Dwyer, K., & Merlin, M. (2020, September 2). *"How Black Students are Becoming Empowered in the Lehigh Valley's Largest, Mostly White Schools".* From Mcall.com: www.mcall.com/news/education/mc-nws-lehigh-valley-black-students-predominantly-white-schools-20200902-35goaqwzyvgilksovptuuueoia-story.html.

Esfandiari, S. (2020, January 16). *"A 17-Year-Old Intern at NASA Discovered a New Planet on His 3rd Day on the Job"*. From Business Insider: www.businessinsider.com/nasa-intern-wolf-cukier-new-planet-third-day-2020-1

Gazzaniga, M. S. (2011). *Who's in Charge?: Free Will and the Science of the Brain.* HarperCollins .

Gould, B., & Kaplan, S. (2020, October 7). *Depth and Complexity Digital Products.* From J Taylor Education: https://www.jtayloreducation.com/digital-depth-complexity-and-content-imperative-products/

Hattie, J. (2018, March). *Hattie Ranking: 252 Influences and Effect Sizes Related to Student Achievement.* From Visible Learning Plus: https://visible-learn-ing.org/hattie-ranking-influences-effect-sizes-learning-achievement/

Heuser, B. L., & Shahid, K. W. (2017). *"Global Dimensions of Gifted and Talented Education: The Influence of National Perceptions on Policies and Practices"*. From ERIC: files.eric.ed.gov/fulltext/EJ1137994.pdf

Hroub, H. a. (2016, September 22). *Education as a Human Right: An Evening with Hanan Al Hroub.* From YouTube/Harvard Graduate School of Education: https://youtu.be/g4lANwTA22k

Hroub, H. a. (2016, 2 17). *Teaching for Peace in Palenstine.* From YouTube: https://youtu.be/g4gVsnyG3rE

Hunt, B. (2017, April). *"The Horse in Motion"*. From Epsilon Theory: https://www.epsilontheory.com/the-horse-in-motion/

Hunter, R., & Hunter, M. C. (2004). *Madeline Hunter's Mastery Teaching: Increasing Instructional Effectiveness in Elementary and Secondary Schools.* Corwin Press.

Johnson, L. (2005). *Teaching Outside the Box: How to Grab Your Students by Their Brains.* Jossey-Bass.

Karimova, H. (2021, May 20). *The Emotion Wheel: What It Is and How to Use It.* From Positive Psychology: https://positivepsychology.com/emotion-wheel/

Leslie, M. (2020). "The Vexing legacy of Lewis Terman". *Stanford Magazine.*

Lind, S. (2011). *Overexcitability and the Gifted.* From SENG: Supporting Emotional Needs of the Gifted: https://www.sengifted.org/post/overexcitability-and-the-gifted

Marzano, R. J. (2019). *The Handbook for the New Art and Science of Teaching*. Solution Tree.

Mathews, J. (1988). *Escalante: The Best Teacher in America*. Henry Holt & Co, Owl Division.

Mazlish, A. F. (1980). *How to Talk So Kids Will Listen and Listen So Kids Will Talk*. New York: Avon.

McGonigal, J. (2011). *Reality is Broken: Why Games Make Us Better and How They Can Change the World*. London: Penguin Press.

McLeod, S. A. (2020, August 5). *Simply Psychology*. From Lev Vygotsky: https://www.simplypsychology.org/vygotsky.html

Mills, J. (2020, January). *"Tips for Making Sure Your New Yar's Resolutions Stick"*. From The Times Tribune: https://www.thetimestribune.com/news/local_news/tips-for-making-sure-your-new-years-resolutions-stick/article_8cd14b54-17fd-51a9-ab5a-89859e6e34c4.html

Mission. (2021). From Technology Student Association : https://tsaweb.org/about/about-tsa/mission

Morin, A. (2014). *13 Things Mentally Strong People Don't Do*. Harper Collins.

Naisbitt, J. (1982). *Megatrends: Ten New Directions Transforming Our Lives*. Macdonald.

Perls, F. S., Hefferline, R. F., & Goodman, P. (2013). *Gestalt Therapy: Excitement and Growth in the Human Personality*. Souvenir Press.

Peters, S., Rambo-Hernandez, K., Makel, M., Matthews, M., & Plucker, J. (2019, May 14). *"Local Norms Improve Equity in Gifted Identification"*. From National Association for Gifted Children: www.nagc.org/blog/local-norms-improve-equity-gifted-identification

Pink, D. H. (2009). *Drive: The Surprising Truth about What Motivates sU*. New York: Riverhead Books.

Plato. (2012, June). *Phaedo (R. Hackforth Edition)*. From Cambridge University Press: https://doi.org/10.1017/CBO9780511620287

Play. (2021, July 1). From Oxford Lexico: https://www.lexico.com/definition/play

Preston, B., & Fisher, B. (1972). Will it Go Round in Circles [Recorded by B. Preston]. Santa Monica, CA, USA.

Ratey, J. J., & Hagerman, E. (2008). *Spark: The Revolutionary New Science of Exercise and the Brain.* Little Brown & Company.

Raymond, C. (2016, November 28). *"20 in Their 20's—Olivia Hallisey.* From Crain's New York Business: www.crainsnewyork.com/awards/olivia-hallisey

Reis, S. M. (2016). *Curriculum Compacting: A Guide to Differentiating Curriculum and Instruction through Enrichment and Acceleration.* Prufrock Press Inc.

Reis, S. M., & Renzulli, J. S. (2005). *Curriculum Compacting: An Easy Start to Differentiating for High-Potential Students.* Prufrock Press.

Renzulli, J. S. (1984). *"The Three Ring Conception of Giftedness: A Developmental Model for Creative Productivity.* From ERIC Clearinghouse: https://eric.ed.gov/?id=EJ418244

Robinson, K., & Aronica, L. (2010). *The Element: How Finding Your Passion Changes Everything.* Penguin.

Sagan, C., & Wageningen, G. v. (1981). *Cosmos.* Van Holkema and Warendorf.

Sanger, S. (2018, July 8). *"The Illusion of Control".* From World of Psychology: psychcentral.com/blog/the-illusion-of-control/

Siegel, D. J. (2012). *Mindsight: Change Your Brain and Your Life.* Scribe Publications.

Siegle, D. (2007, November 30). *National Alliance for Gifted Children.* From Gifted Children's Bill of Rights: https://www.nagc.org/resources-publications/resources-parents/gifted-childrens-bill-rights

Sinek, S. (2013). *Start With Why: How Great Leaders Inspire Everyone to Take Action.* Porfolio/Penguin.

Smith, J. N. (Director). (1995). *Dangerous Minds* [Motion Picture].

Strauss, V. (2014, June 4). *"Why Hedge Funds Love Charter Schools.* From The Washington Post: https://www.washingtonpost.com/news/answer-sheet/wp/2014/06/04/why-hedge-funds-love-charter-schools/

Taylor, C. (2020, August 27). *The Probability of Rolling a Yahtzee.* From ThoughtCo: https://www.thoughtco.com/probability-of-rolling-a-yahtzee-3126593

Teacher Compensation. (2021, May 5). From United States Department of Education: https://www.ed.gov/oii-news/teacher-compensation

Terada, Y. (2018, March). *"Research-Tested Benefit of Breaks Reducing Stress".* From Edutopia: https://www.edutopia.org/article/research-tested-benefits-breaks#:~:text=Research-Tested%20Benefits%20of%20Breaks%201%20Reducing%20Stress%2C%20Increasing,...%20 4%20Incorporating%20Breaks%20in%20Your%20Classroom.%20

Terman, L. M. (1916). *The Measurement of Intelligence: An Explanation of and a Complete Guide for the Use of th STandord Revision and Extension of the Binet-Simon Intelligence Scale.* Boston, MA: Houghton-Mifflin.

Thoreau, H. D. (2020, July 15). *"On the Duty of Civil Disobedience".* From The Project Gutenberg EBook: www.gutenberg.org/files/71/71h/71-h.htm

Tillier, W. (2009, March 26). "Dabrowski Without the Theory of Positive Disintegration Just Isn't Dabrowski. *Roeper Review*, pp. 123-126.

Tim. (2015, November 20). *What is Player Agency and What is it Good For?* From RPG Stackexchange: https://rpg.stackexchange.com/questions/71265/what-is-player-agency-and-what-is-it-good-for

Tomlinson, C. A. (2018). *How to Differentiate Instruction in Academically Diverse Classrooms.* Echo Point Books and Media LLC.

Vialle, W., & Ziegler, A. (2016). *"Gifted Education in Modern Asia: Analyses from a Systemic Perspective.".* University of Wollongong Australia. From University of Wollongong Australia.

Watters, J. (2017, July 20). *Contextualising learning in STEM.* From World Gifted: https://www.world-gifted.org/WCGTC17-Presentations/K1.pdf

What is Giftedness. (2019, March). From National Alliance for Gifted Children: http://www.nagc.org/resources-publications/resources/what-giftedness

Wiggins, G., & McTighe, J. (1998). *Understanding by Design.* ASCD.

Yee, N. (2014). *The Protues Paradox: How Online Games and Virtual Worlds Change Us—and How They Don't.* Yale University Press.

CPSIA information can be obtained
at www.ICGtesting.com
Printed in the USA
BVHW072011140722
641967BV00002B/3